DE HAVILLAND
TIGER MOTH

1931–1945 (all marks)

First published in July 2009

A catalogue record for this book is available from the
British Library

ISBN 978 1 84425 586 3

Library of Congress control no. 2008943627

Published by Haynes Publishing,
Sparkford, Yeovil, Somerset BA22 7JJ, UK
Tel: 01963 442030 Fax: 01963 440001
Int. tel: +44 1963 442030 Int. fax: +44 1963 440001
E-mail: sales@haynes.co.uk
Website: www.haynes.co.uk

Haynes North America Inc.
861 Lawrence Drive, Newbury Park,
California 91320, USA

Printed and bound in the UK

ACKNOWLEDGEMENTS

de Havilland Moth Club
Stuart McKay MBE
Mike Vaisey
Paul Sharman
Dennis Neville
Vintage Engine Technology Limited
Ian Castle
Matthew Boddington
Dr. Mark Miller
De Havilland Support Limited
Bryn Hughes
Geoff Collins
Brian A. Marshall
Andy Smith
Frank Long
Bob Gibson
Ken Peters
Andy Saunders
Geoff Chennells
Arthur Mason
Doreen Gillman
Cathy Silk
Terry Holloway, Marshall Aerospace
Cambridge Flying Group
Nick Bloom, Pilot Magazine
Michael Oakey, Aeroplane Monthly
Bill Ison
Barry Tempest
Chris Parker
Lewis Benjamin
Bruno Vonlanthen

… and the many other members of the
deHMC who have patiently submitted to
my poking, prodding and asking dumb
questions over the past year!

DE HAVILLAND TIGER MOTH

1931–1945 (all marks)

Owners' Workshop Manual

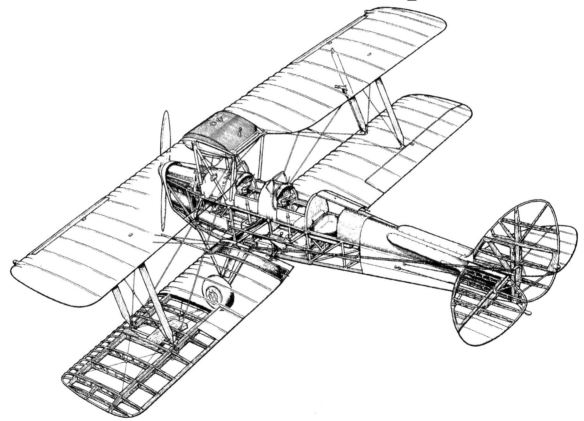

An insight into owning, flying and maintaining
the legendary British training biplane

Stephen Slater
with the assistance of the de Havilland Moth Club

Contents

6 Introduction

16 The Tiger Moth story

Tiger's tale	17
Primarily, a military trainer	23
Mass production	29
Peacetime, retirement, work…and play	33
The de Havilland Moth Club	38
Sir Geoffrey de Havilland	40

44 Anatomy of the Tiger Moth

Under the skin	45
Engine	53
Fuel system	61
Ignition system	63
Fuselage	64
Undercarriage	67
Traditional woodwork	70
Fabric covering	74
Rigging, flying and landing wires	76
Propeller	78
Wood – nature's composite	81
Wood repairs	85
Fabric repairs	85

88 The owner's view

Owning and enjoying a Tiger Moth	89
Flying for fun	94
Buying a Tiger	101

104 The pilot's view

Taming the Tiger	105
Cockpit check	109
Climb aboard	110
Walk-around check	113
Chocks away	114
Time to go flying	116
Tricks of the trade	119
The right stuff	122
A wartime student's-eye view	124

128 The engineer's view

An engineer's aeroplane	129
Routine maintenance	132
Daily inspections	132
50-hour and 100-hour checks	134
Deep maintenance	138
'All aeroplanes bite fools'	140
Tiger toolkit	140

142 Epilogue

146 Appendices

Moth ancestors and variants	146
How many were built, and how many survive?	153
Glossary and abbreviations	154
Useful contacts	155

158 Index

LEFT: **There are few sights and sounds as timeless in the world of aviation as a Tiger Moth returning home on a summer's evening.** *(Geoff Collins)*

'A Tiger Moth is the ideal trainer. Easy to fly, but blooming difficult to fly well!'

Bill Ison
Tiger Moth Instructor for over 60 years

Introduction

The de Havilland Tiger Moth is that rarest of things, an object which means all things to all people. One may admire the fragile beauty of its dragonfly shape against an azure sky, while another will give thanks for the resilience of that same structure, as a student pilot finds its handling to be challenging to the point of confusion. For another more mature aviator, the Tiger Moth may bring back memories of adventures and old comrades long gone.

LEFT: Seeking that elusive 'daisy cutter' landing is a timeless challenge, enjoyed by Tiger Moth pilots for over three-quarters of a century. *(Geoff Collins)*

RIGHT: The Tiger Moth was critical in providing the cadre of pilots that fought – and won – the Battle of Britain. *(Geoff Collins)*

BELOW: 1938 shot of Hatfield Reserve Flying School DH82A, **L6923.** *(RAF Museum via deHMC Archive)*

Some find the open cockpit intimate, others find it draughty, but bracing nonetheless. For some the Tiger Moth is a hard-working, reliable, tool of the trade, while for others it is a means of escape from the world below. Some eagerly anticipate watching the world unfold beneath the wings, struts and bracing wires, while others revel in turning that same horizon upside down with a loop and a roll on a summer's afternoon.

Although built and flown around the world, the Tiger Moth is traditional Britishness personified. It sits with the Last Night of the Proms, vintage Bentleys, rugby at Twickenham, cricket on the village green and flagons of old ale. Someone once said that if a Tiger Moth is fitted with a radio, it automatically seeks the BBC Home Service.

Yet the Tiger Moth is more than an anachronism. Park a Tiger Moth on the flight line of any airport and it draws attention and

respect. There is still no shortage of pilots who wish to learn its foibles, and passengers who clamour to occupy the front seat once occupied by the instructor.

For over seven decades the Tiger Moth has survived wars, dereliction and legislation, as well as the hazards of the air. It is a truly remarkable survivor and is probably, justifiably, the most famous biplane ever built.

Even at the peak of its service life in World War Two, the Tiger Moth was something of an anachronism. It was a biplane trainer in an era of monoplane fighters and multi-engined bombers. Yet the pilots trained on it went on to fly Spitfires, Hurricanes and Lancasters. Not to mention airliners and the first generations of supersonic jets.

The Tiger Moth is working proof that good design can stand the test of time. Around 650 remain airworthy, continuing to offer a true vintage flying experience, in all its open-cockpit glory.

BELOW: The Tiger Nine formation team overfly Stonehenge on a practice flight in the summer of 2008. At the top of the picture is the former RAF station at Larkhill, which in 1912 became Britain's first military airfield. *(Geoff Collins)*

OPPOSITE: R5130 captured by a Hatfield staff photographer on a flight from the airfield in June 1940. *(deHMC archive)*

There can be few sights and sounds as timeless in the world of aviation as watching a de Havilland Tiger Moth return to base on a summer's evening. First the tractor-like bark of its exhaust breaks the birdsong. Then the biplane silhouette grows steadily larger against the lowering sun.

The Tiger Moth next shows its distinctive profile, as the pilot joins the circuit to land with an 'overhead join', itself a tradition of safe arrival at non-radio airfields stretching back to World War One. It is followed by a gentle pop-pop from the exhausts as the pilot throttles back, judging the circuit to give a gently side-slipped approach to (the pilot hopes) a perfect three-point arrival.

While the scenario seems almost too good to be true, the Tiger Moth continues to offer this ageless experience to pilots and spectators alike over three-quarters of a century after the first examples took to the air.

The Tiger Moth story begins in a period viewed by many as the 'golden era' of flying, with no radios, uninhibited adventures and almost no air traffic control. Geoffrey de Havilland was one of Britain's true aviation pioneers, who began to build his first design in 1909.

De Havilland's business was built on the success of the DH60 Moth, which first flew in 1925. Over 1,000 examples of different variants were built and it became the most popular light aircraft in the world.

From it was evolved the Tiger Moth, which made its first flight on 26 October 1931. It was designed primarily as a military variant, with a more robust fuselage and more powerful engine than the DH60.

The Tiger Moth's distinctive 'swept wing' appearance was also dictated by military requirements. The upper wing was moved forward and the wings swept back to maintain the centre of gravity, while allowing the instructor to more easily exit the front cockpit in an emergency while wearing a bulky parachute.

As war clouds began to form, the Tiger Moth became critical to providing the cadre of RAF pilots that fought and won the Battle of Britain.

BELOW: Recreating the golden era of flight. *(Geoff Collins)*

ABOVE: **Hatfield production line, 1939.** *(deHMC archive)*

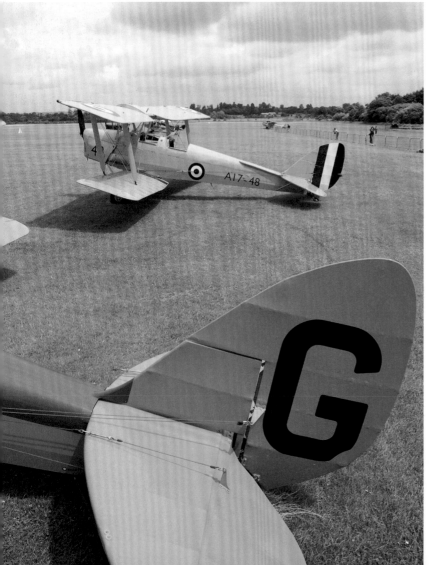

LEFT: **In contrast to the camouflage of British wartime Tiger Moths, many of those in Australia carried a high-visibility all-yellow finish.** *(Geoff Collins)*

It went on to train hundreds of thousands of aircrew in the UK, Canada, India, Australia, New Zealand and Africa.

For more than two decades after the war the Tiger Moth continued as the basis of flying clubs, air taxi services, flying schools and crop-spraying businesses around the world. Of the just over 8,000 built, it is estimated that 1,000 examples survive. Of those, about 650 are believed to be in airworthy condition. Adding to this truly amazing survival rate, newly rebuilt examples continue to return to the air.

A key to the Tiger Moth's remarkable ability to survive is the elegant simplicity of its design, the roots of which date back to the 1914–18 conflict. With its mostly wooden structure covered with doped fabric, it is surprisingly robust and, if damaged, relatively straightforward to repair.

Additionally, the de Havilland Gipsy range

LEFT: As G-ANFM and this Bristol Fighter demonstrate, the Tiger Moth's construction and design dates back to World War One.
(Stephen Slater)

BELOW: The reliable Gipsy Major engine remains a prime reason for the Tiger Moth's success.
(deHMC archive)

of engines marked a breakthrough in the development of light aircraft power units. At the time of the Gipsy's introduction in the late 1920s, the manufacture of an engine which operated for 100 flying hours without major overhaul was a noteworthy achievement.

The legendary reliability of the de Havilland Gipsy Major engine transformed such thinking. It was the first engine to offer a service life of 1,000 hours – and that has subsequently been extended based on experience in service. There are several Tiger Moths today flying behind engines that, thanks to regular inspections and careful routine maintenance, have flown for several 'lifetimes'.

One of the major attractions of the Tiger Moth to many pilots today is that its flying characteristics provide an authentic, yet still safe, challenge to their flying skills. The aircraft's control responses are far from perfect and there is absolute truth in the old adage that 'A Tiger Moth is easy to fly, but incredibly hard to fly well'.

It was precisely those characteristics which made it such a superb trainer in its day. Some other contemporary training types offered greater control harmony and more benign handling than the Tiger Moth, but its genius is sometimes said to be the fact that it reproduced the handling

OPPOSITE: 'Papa Kilo' has been based at Sywell aerodrome in Northamptonshire for almost 20 years. It carries the livery worn by Brooklands Aviation Tiger Moths when they flew from the same airfield in the 1930s. *(Ian Castle)*

quirks of many more powerful and complex military types, but in a way and at a speed that a student pilot could begin to master.

In particular these characteristics manifest themselves in landing and ground handling. The combination of narrow-tracked undercarriage and a high centre of gravity, created by the mounting of the fuel tank in the centre-section of the upper wing, demands accurate control.

However, the relative inefficiency of the ailerons makes that difficult – and the combination of the forward-set undercarriage and sensitive elevator control is always there to humiliate the unwary, inaccurate or simply unlucky, with a spectacular bounce! Add in restricted forward vision during taxiing, landing and take-off, and it can be seen why pilots trained on modern aeroplanes have to go 'back to school' to learn the Tiger's traits.

Along the way, they learn operating practices first developed during the Great War. The starting procedure, with its 'flooding' of the carburettor when cold, followed by the routine of 'switches off, sucking in', 'contact' and, if necessary on an over-primed engine, 'blowing out', all demand a close rapport with the propeller swinger.

Once started, the Tiger Moth pilot and ground crew once again revert to practices honed on aeroplanes such as the Sopwith Camel. In the absence of any wheel brakes, engine checks are carried out while the aeroplane still has its chocks in place.

Once the 'chocks away' signal is given, steering is then carried out with bursts of power blowing air over the rudder, partially aided by a steerable cast-iron tailskid and, when required, by 'wing-walkers' applying gentle pressure to the wing tips.

This need for more careful ground handling than on modern types of aircraft becomes particularly acute when faced with airports. The Tiger Moth's design predates hard, tarmac runways and concrete aprons, and it was originally flown from large grass aerodromes where the aircraft were simply aligned into the prevailing wind for take-off and landing. The need for crosswind landings which came with the introduction of designated runways adds yet another challenge to those trying to 'tame' a Tiger.

Some owners today follow the practice of the Royal Canadian Air Force, who from the outset fitted their Tiger Moths with main-wheel brakes and a steerable tail-wheel instead of the heavy metal tailskid of the original design. Other owners prefer to meet the challenge by developing their piloting skills to cope with all eventualities.

Recent sister editions of Haynes Manuals have focussed on aeroplanes such as the Vickers Supermarine Spitfire and the Avro Lancaster, which are the domain of a privileged few, unattainable to mere mortals. In contrast, examples of the de Havilland Tiger Moth are still regularly bought and sold today.

The Tiger Moth's RAF service career came to an end in 1952, when the final examples in RAF Volunteer Reserve Squadrons were replaced by another de Havilland basic training type, the Chipmunk. By then there was already an established civilian 'trade' in Tiger Moths, catering for demobbed pilots who had trained on the type, supported by military-trained engineers who had learned their craft of maintaining and repairing them during their National Service.

While the legend of the 'ten pound Tiger Moths' has never been proved, serviceable military surplus aeroplanes were often sold for as little as £50 after the war. They formed the basis of flying clubs, air taxi services, flying schools, and glider-towing and crop-spraying businesses all around the world.

Today, depending on condition, an airworthy Tiger Moth can most likely be purchased in the

BELOW: Teamwork between the propeller swinger and the pilot remains vital for safety, both then and now. *(deHMC archive)*

UK for between £40,000 and £60,000. In terms of cost, it places the aeroplane at the level of a reasonably exotic classic car.

Of course, the levels of maintenance are stricter and more time-consuming than for most automotive classics. Many private owners, though, relish the tactile pleasures of working with a piece of living aviation history. They successfully operate Tiger Moths from small airfields and private farm strips, handling much of the routine maintenance themselves, under the supervision of authorised aircraft engineers.

However, we are duty-bound to remind readers that this manual is no substitute for the 120-plus closely-typed pages that make up the original de Havilland Maintenance and Repair Manuals. These manuals remain the definitive source of maintenance information. We hope that this book will act as an additional and enjoyable resource, but only the official manuals should be used as the maintenance reference for those working on the type.

BELOW: Formation take-off by RAF VR Tiger Moths. *(deHMC archive)*

'Although built and flown around the world, the Tiger Moth is traditional Britishness personified...'

Chapter One

The Tiger Moth story

Tiger's tale

On 26 October 1931 the prototype DH82 Tiger Moth made its first flight from the company's Stag Lane airfield at Edgware on the northern outskirts of London. However, the story that led to the creation of the iconic biplane began more than a decade earlier.

Geoffrey de Havilland had made his name initially as a designer at the Royal Aircraft Factory, Farnborough, then moved on to create military aeroplanes carrying first the name Airco, then his own company name. Business boomed, as the DH4 and DH9 light bombers proved to be two of the most successful aeroplanes of the type during the First World War, but the post-Armistice market was flooded by a glut of cheap surplus aeroplanes and the company was left running on a shoestring.

He was sure, however, there was a strong potential for a 'private-owner' aeroplane. The government thought so too, and the Air Ministry along with the Royal Aero Club, created a series of trials for lightweight aircraft in 1923 and 1924.

However, the trials were based on a flawed precept. The

LEFT: G-ANFM, based at White Waltham in Berkshire, continues a tradition of Tiger Moth operations at the airfield which began when they were used by the wartime ferry pilots of the Air Transport Auxiliary. *(Andy Smith)*

rules permitted only small engines of limited horsepower, which meant that the participants were little more than powered gliders. Although de Havilland had designed one of the more successful aircraft in the trials, the DH53 Humming Bird, he had already realised that a larger, more robust aeroplane would be more practical.

His first truly practical private-owner aeroplane was the DH51 biplane. Larger and heavier than the Moths which were to be its successors, it was designed around war surplus Royal Aircraft Factory V-8 engines, based on those previously used in de Havilland's BE2 reconnaissance design and DH6 trainer. While the big air-cooled V-8 engine driving a huge four-bladed propeller of some 8ft 9in (2.67m) was heavy and thirsty, it had one big advantage: its price. De Havilland had negotiated with the Aircraft Disposal Company, Airdisco, to buy the engines for just 25 shillings (£1.25) each!

However, the size and cost of operation of the DH51 was not much less than a converted military type and just three were sold, so de Havilland sought a new compromise. He began discussions with Major Frank Halford, a freelance engine designer who worked for Airdisco, regarding the viability of turning one half of the '25-bob' engine into a low-cost four-cylinder unit. The price would also be kept down by using magnetos and carburettors fitted to popular cars.

Halford's new engine mounted four of the Airdisco cylinders vertically on a custom-made crankcase, which contained a sump for the lubricating oil, as in an automobile engine. From its displacement of 4.05 litres it developed 65hp at a peak of just over 2,000rpm. More importantly, it weighed a mere 286lb (130kg). It became known as the ADC Cirrus.

Around this new engine de Havilland created a simple, conventional biplane, along the lines of a scaled-down DH51. Ease of construction, repair and operation were priorities, with a plywood box fuselage and straight, unstaggered wings which could be folded along the fuselage sides for ease of hangarage.

In the centre section of the upper wing, above the two cockpits, an aerodynamically shaped 15-gallon (68-litre) fuel tank provided a gravity-feed to the engine for three hours' flying and removed any need for fuel pumps. Meanwhile, there were no metal mountings to hold the engine in place, it being bolted instead directly on to the fuselage longerons. With the exception of metal tubes used to form the distinctive curvature of the wingtips, elevators and rudder, all the flying surfaces were of linen-covered wooden construction.

De Havilland aimed the new aeroplane squarely at the enthusiastic amateur and weekend flyer and therefore decided that a name would be more appropriate than a type number. The choice came from his lifelong interest in nature, in particular Lepidoptera, the study of moths.

RIGHT: G-EBKT, the first DH60 Moth, made its maiden flight in the hands of Geoffrey de Havilland on 22 February 1925. *(deHMC archive)*

'It suddenly struck me that the name Moth was just right,' wrote de Havilland in his autobiography, *Sky Fever*. 'It had the right sound, was appropriate, easy to remember and might well lead to a series of Moths, all named after British insects.'

A new era of private flying began on the chilly Sunday afternoon of 22 February 1925, when Geoffrey de Havilland, having enjoyed his regular Sunday lunch with his family, climbed aboard the prototype Moth G-EBKT and, with minimal fanfare, lifted off from the muddy turf of the de Havilland airfield at Stag Lane.

The Moth was a classic example of being in the right place at the right time, and 'hit the spot' with potential buyers. It was almost £100 cheaper than equivalent types such as the Avro Avian and Blackburn Bluebird, and its costs of upkeep were similarly economical.

Equally important was the fact that it had sufficient (and reliable) power to carry two people plus fuel and luggage, making it a practical workhorse. Such was the Moth's success that Director of Civil Aviation Sir Sefton Brancker authorised their purchase as the prime equipment of the Air Ministry-sponsored flying clubs which were being created around the United Kingdom, ultimately ordering a total of 90 examples.

A new engine

Frank Halford further refined the ADC Cirrus engine, reducing its weight by 30lb (13.6kg) while at the same time increasing its power output to 80hp. De Havilland, though, was aware that he was too dependent on Airdisco's rapidly diminishing stock of war-surplus components. He therefore decided to invest in his own aero-engine production line and commissioned Halford to design an engine which would be purpose-made for the job.

The resulting de Havilland Gipsy I was in many ways similar to the Cirrus. It was still mounted vertically as in an automobile, with the four air-cooled cylinders sitting atop the crankcase and sump, but it now turned anti-clockwise when viewed from the cockpit, the opposite direction to the Cirrus. While slightly heavier at 300lb (136kg), it developed more power and would subsequently surpass even the Cirrus in terms of reliability.

ABOVE: In 1929 Arthur Marshall created a new airfield at Cambridge for a growing fleet of DH60 Moths. A spectacular Moth air race was one of the opening event attractions. *(Marshall Aviation via deHMC)*

A Tiger Moth – but not as we know it

In order to test the new engine, de Havilland first fitted it not into a Moth, but into an all-new single-seat racing aeroplane, the DH71. Two examples of this high-speed test-bed were built. Although they bore no resemblance to the subsequent biplane, they were the first aircraft to bear the name Tiger Moth.

In racing tune, as fitted to the DH71, the Gipsy I developed 135hp at 2,650rpm and gave the diminutive monoplane a top speed faster than RAF fighter aircraft of the period. In August 1927 the DH71 Tiger Moth set a new world light aircraft speed record, covering a 100km circuit at an average of 186.5mph (298 kph). An attempt on the world altitude record was only abandoned at 19,190ft (5,849m) due to a lack of oxygen for the pilot, with the aircraft still climbing furiously.

These full-throttle test flights led to unprecedented levels of reliability for the new engine. When the first production Gipsy I engine was fitted to the Moth airframe in the summer of 1928 it was detuned to a relatively under-stressed 98hp at 1,900rpm. As a publicity exercise an early example was sealed and flown for an unprecedented 600 hours with only routine maintenance.

A new model of the Moth was named the DH60G Gipsy Moth and thereafter the ADC-powered aeroplanes were retrospectively known as Cirrus Moths and, if fitted with the uprated ADC engine, as Hermes Moths. The Gipsy Moth became a household name in May 1930 following the epic 19-day flight by Amy Johnson

TOP: Built purely as a test bed, the DH71 was the first aeroplane to carry the title 'Tiger Moth'. Test pilot Hubert Broad runs up the engine prior to flight. *(deHMC archive)*

CENTRE: Geoffrey de Havilland Jr at Leicester in September 1929, with just a few hours remaining on the unprecedented 600-hour reliability test. *(deHMC archive)*

LEFT: The DH60 Moth became a familiar sight during the 1930s, both in the air and on the ground. *(Stephen Slater)*

in her Gipsy Moth 'Jason', to become the first woman to fly solo from Britain to Australia.

The Gipsy Moth would become the most numerous example of the early Moth line. By 1934, over 1,100 DH60 variants had been built at Stag Lane, as well as licensed examples being built in Australia, France, Norway, Sweden and the United States. It was, quite simply, the most popular light aircraft in the world.

In 1928 the DH60M – or Metal Moth, as it became known – was introduced for markets where the use of a wooden fuselage was impractical either in terms of strength or climate. It utilised the fabric-covered, welded steel-tube construction which would later be used in the Tiger Moth, and it found particular favour in Canada, Australia and the United States, where it was produced in factories of de Havilland associated companies.

In 1931 an additional variant of the DH60M was marketed for military training as the DH60T Moth Trainer. It continued to feature an upright installation, but the Gipsy engine was increased in capacity from 5.2 to 5.7 litres, producing 120hp.

At the same time, de Havilland developed a new installation of the Gipsy engine for a new touring monoplane, the Puss Moth. Endeavouring to improve its forward view and provide a cleaner engine cowling, the engine was converted to a 'dry sump' design with a

remote oil tank feeding the engine via a suction pump. This allowed it to be fitted inverted, with the cylinders suspended below the crankcase.

When fitted with the resulting Gipsy III power unit, the wooden-fuselaged Moth was redesignated the DH60GIII and for the first time demonstrated the distinctive nose profile later associated with the Tiger Moth. Some metal-fuselaged aircraft supplied as military trainers to the Swedish Air Force with Gipsy III engines were redesignated the DH60T Tiger Moth.

In Britain, although the Royal Air Force had used around 100 DH60 Moth aircraft on limited training and liaison duties, basic flying training was still being carried out on the heavier and

ABOVE: Between them, de Havilland test pilot Hubert Broad and racer Wally Hope won the King's Cup air race with DH Moths in 1926, 1927 and 1928. *(deHMC archive)*

BELOW: The RAF was unhappy that the unswept wings and upright engine of the DH60 Moth restricted visibility and cockpit access. *(Geoff Collins)*

These two engine diagrams show the change in installation which provided an improved forward view and cleaner cowling design for the Moth Major and Tiger Moth.

(Rolls-Royce Heritage Trust)

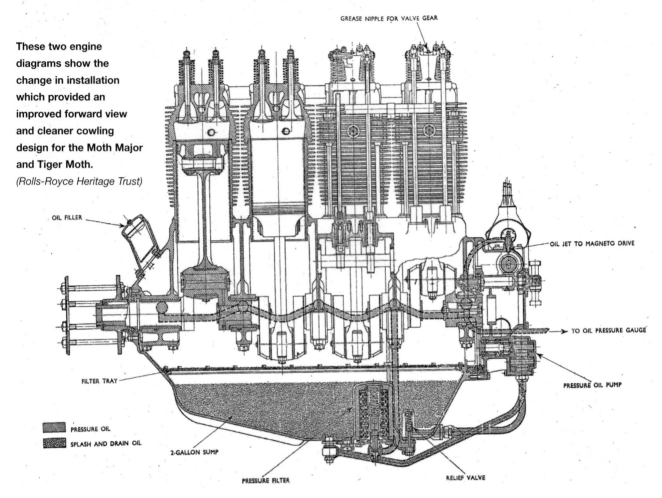

GREASE NIPPLE FOR VALVE GEAR

OIL FILLER

OIL JET TO MAGNETO DRIVE

TO OIL PRESSURE GAUGE

PRESSURE OIL PUMP

FILTER TRAY

PRESSURE OIL

SPLASH AND DRAIN OIL

2-GALLON SUMP

PRESSURE FILTER

RELIEF VALVE

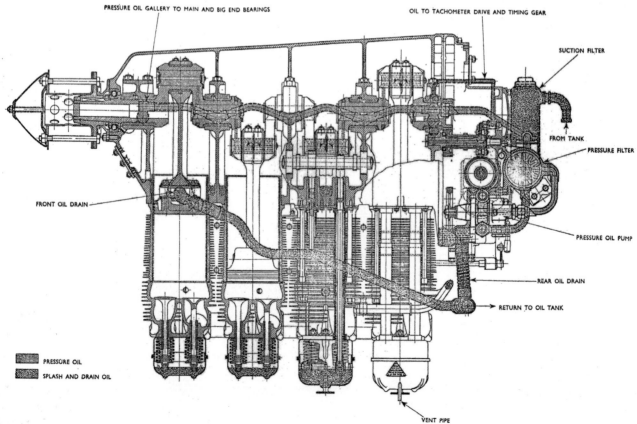

PRESSURE OIL GALLERY TO MAIN AND BIG END BEARINGS

OIL TO TACHOMETER DRIVE AND TIMING GEAR

SUCTION FILTER

FROM TANK

PRESSURE FILTER

FRONT OIL DRAIN

PRESSURE OIL PUMP

REAR OIL DRAIN

RETURN TO OIL TANK

PRESSURE OIL

SPLASH AND DRAIN OIL

VENT PIPE

more expensive to operate Avro Tutor. Though the RAF wished to standardise on a new, more economical training type, one of its concerns regarding the use of the Moth was the difficulty in vacating the front instructor's seat in an emergency. With the 'straight-wing' Moths, the fuel tank, struts and wing above the seat left only a narrow gap through which to squeeze into the front cockpit. Consequently the combination of heavy military clothing and compulsory parachute made it unlikely that an instructor could safely escape a damaged aeroplane.

Geoffrey de Havilland admitted later to 'expending many hours' on the conundrum of how to move the upper wings away from the cockpit without the lift from the wings being too far ahead of the centre of gravity. Ultimately the solution came not on a drawing board, but by a process of evolution.

In a small shed on Stag Lane aerodrome, designer Arthur Hagg, project engineer Douglas Hunter and a handful of engineers dismantled a DH60T Moth Trainer for use as a full-scale mock-up. It is recorded that initially the centre section was moved forward 18in (450mm) to improve the cockpit access. Then, after pondering the matter over lunch, de Havilland and test pilot Hubert Broad advocated moving it a further 4in (100mm). That, however, now placed the cabane strut mountings on an unbraced section of fuselage longeron, so a new braced pickup joint was created.

Now came the thorny problem of re-establishing the centre of gravity. Out came the slide rules and pencils. The calculations indicated that sweeping back both pairs of wings until the interplane struts were 9in (225mm) behind their original position would restore the status quo.

This was duly achieved by producing a set of new spruce rear wing spars with their inner ends shortened by 3in (75mm) and adjusting the fittings to suit. However, when the wings were fitted the centre of gravity stubbornly remained outside its limits.

Reluctant to sacrifice yet another pair of expensive lower rear spars, the team instead increased the sweepback of the upper wings by a further 2in (50mm). Thus was born the distinctive outline of the Tiger Moth, with unequal sweepback of upper and lower wings.

Perhaps in the interests of keeping paperwork to a minimum, the first eight examples of the type were not classed as a new type at all, but were merely regarded as a modification of the DH60T design. However, the Air Ministry's naming policy of the time indicated that the type should have a name beginning with the letter 'T', so, in line with Avro's Tutor and Hawker's Tomtit, the revised Moth gained its name: de Havilland Tiger Moth.

ABOVE: By moving the wing centre-section forward, access and egress is significantly simplified. *(deHMC)*

Primarily, a military trainer

The DH60T Tiger Moth test aircraft 'E-5', later G-ABNJ, was delivered by Hubert Broad on 18 August 1931 for evaluation by the Armament and Aeroplane Experimental Establishment at Martlesham Heath in Suffolk. An early response from the unit was favourable, but highlighted the fact that the wing sweepback now placed the lower wingtips closer to the ground, and that there was a likelihood of the ailerons striking the ground while taxiing.

This was remedied by increasing the level of dihedral to 4.5° on the lower wings of the second aeroplane, G-ABPH, which was delivered to Martlesham Heath on 3 September. At the end of the month a formal Air Ministry contract was placed for an initial batch of 35 aircraft.

It was only now that the changes were deemed sufficient to warrant a designation in its own right. Thus, the first 'official' DH82 Tiger Moth flight took place with the maiden flight of G-ABRC on 26 October 1931.

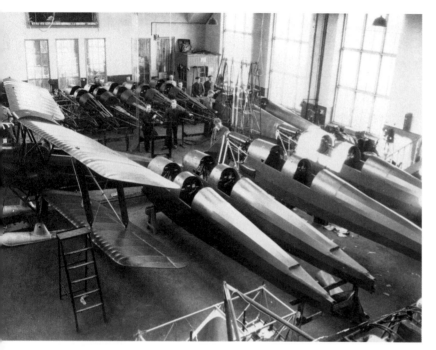

ABOVE: Seventeen DH82 aircraft were built at Kjeller in Norway in 1932 – note the ski undercarriage. *(Oyvind Ellingsen via deHMC)*

was the Swedish Air Force and a licence agreement for future production was granted to A.B. Svensker Järnvagverkstädena, a company whose title was later changed to SAAB.

One of the early British-built DH82s delivered to Sweden is the oldest surviving Tiger Moth in the world. SE-ADF made her first flight on 16 June 1932 and served with the Swedish Air Force until 1945 before being transferred to a civilian flying school.

In 1949, it was acquired by the Royal Swedish Aero Club, the KSAK, who have owned the aeroplane ever since. Originally a hard-working glider tug and training aircraft, SE-ADF was subsequently fully restored and flies as an ambassador for the Aero Club with a second KSAK Tiger Moth, SE-ALM, in a dark grey and orange paint scheme originally designed to contrast with snow-covered Scandinavian backdrops.

While the DH60 Moth and its variants had been primarily marketed as private aeroplanes, the emphasis behind the DH82 Tiger Moth was clearly as a modern military trainer. In the first few years of production only a handful of Tiger Moths were made available to civilian organisations.

One exception to the military bias was the famous record-breaking pilot Sir Alan Cobham. He was allowed to acquire two examples for

Such was the pace of production at Stag Lane that just two weeks later, on November 9, the first six Tiger Moth Mk1 aircraft were picked up by instructors from No 3 Flying Training School for delivery to their base at Grantham in Lincolnshire.

In addition to the Air Ministry contract, export sales boomed. Early DH82s were shipped to Hong Kong, Japan, Norway, Persia, Portugal and Denmark. One of the biggest customers

RIGHT: SE-ADF is the oldest surviving Tiger Moth, delivered to Sweden in 1932. She continues to grace Scandinavian skies today. *(deHMC)*

use in his 'National Aviation Day' displays, which developed aviation awareness across Great Britain.

In addition to making the public even more conscious of the Tiger Moth type, Cobham's 'flying circus' – which visited 300 towns in a season – also provided important feedback on reliability. A contemporary de Havilland advertisement recorded that between April and September 1932, 'a standard Tiger Moth…is estimated to have completed 2,520 landings, 345 bunts (or outside loops), 300 upward rolls, 1,440 loops, 1,080 rolls, inverted loops and approximately 90 hours flying upside down'.

One issue noted with the Gipsy III engine in the DH82 was a tendency to overheat when held in a long, slow climb. This was remedied in 1932 with the introduction of an uprated engine with the capacity raised from 5.71 to 6.12 litres and the power boosted to 130hp at 2,350rpm. The new engine was called the Gipsy Major.

As important as its added power was its unprecedented life. In an era of white metal bearings and relatively poor quality lubrication, major aero-engine overhauls every 100 hours were commonplace, and even the Gipsy I, itself a paragon of reliability, had an overhaul life of only 300 hours. Consequently a major selling point of the Gipsy Major on its introduction was its overhaul life of 450 hours. By July 1933,

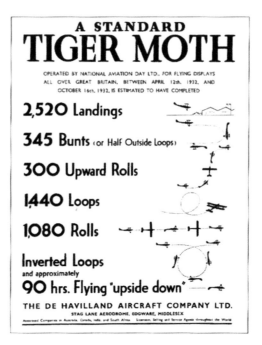

A STANDARD TIGER MOTH

OPERATED BY NATIONAL AVIATION DAY LTD., FOR FLYING DISPLAYS ALL OVER GREAT BRITAIN, BETWEEN APRIL 12th, 1932, AND OCTOBER 16th, 1932, IS ESTIMATED TO HAVE COMPLETED

2,520 Landings

345 Bunts (or Half Outside Loops)

300 Upward Rolls

1,440 Loops

1,080 Rolls

Inverted Loops
and approximately
90 hrs. Flying "upside down"

THE DE HAVILLAND AIRCRAFT COMPANY LTD.
STAG LANE AERODROME, EDGWARE, MIDDLESEX
Associated Companies in Australia, Canada, India, and South Africa Licensees, Selling and Service Agents throughout the World

based on experience in service, this had been raised to 750 hours, and in August 1937 de Havilland proudly proclaimed '1,000 hours between overhauls for Gipsy Major engines'.

The first production DH82A Tiger Moth, carrying the civilian registration G-ACDA, was destined to ultimately join the de Havilland School of Flying at the company's new base at Hatfield in Hertfordshire. In March 1933 it was evaluated by the A&AEE at Martlesham Heath,

ABOVE: G-ACDA, the first production DH82A, joined the de Havilland School of Flying at Hatfield in the summer of 1933. *(Geoff Collins)*

BELOW: This well-known Air Ministry publicity shot of R-5130 flying from 1 EFTS at Hatfield in 1939 shows early wartime camouflage. *(deHMC archive)*

leading to an initial RAF order for 50 aeroplanes to be designated the Tiger Moth Mk II.

In addition to the Gipsy Major I power unit, there were a number of airframe refinements. The fuel tank capacity was increased from 18 to 19 gallons (81 to 86 litres) and the front cockpit doors were reduced slightly in size, but the most obvious change was the replacement of the original fabric and stringer top covering of the rear fuselage by a more robust curved top decking made of steamed and moulded plywood.

The Tiger Moths operated by the de Havilland School of Flying, along with other civilian schools around the UK, played a dual role. As well as training and offering flying club facilities to civilian

pilots, the schools were also part of the Royal Air Force Reserve, allowing former RAF pilots to maintain their flying skills. As war clouds loomed, they assumed an increasing role in the grading of prospective pilots as part of the Air Training Plan, which became one of the cornerstones of the pre-war expansion of the RAF.

The logic of the system was that it was significantly faster and cheaper to evaluate initial flying skills at the newly designated Elementary and Reserve Flying Training Schools (ERFTS). Only if the cadets were successful would they then be enrolled in the more complex and formal RAF 12-month pilot training courses.

The eight weeks spent at the ERFTS would give the students around 50 hours' flying time, with the expectation of their achieving their first solo in the first quarter of the course. Those that succeeded were then either offered a Royal Air Force career or remained in their civilian jobs and flew as members of the Royal Air Force Volunteer Reserve (RAFVR).

By 1939 the number of ERFTS had grown to more than 50, supplemented by three University Air Squadrons, at Cambridge, Oxford and London. Almost all were equipped with Tiger Moths. By the time that war was declared in September 1939 around 1,400 were in service and the de Havilland factory at Hatfield was delivering 40 aeroplanes a week.

With the outbreak of war a reorganisation saw the civilian-run ERFTS incorporated into 30 Elementary Flying Training Schools (EFTS) under Air Ministry control. The instruction process was little changed, however, with the same instructors and the same aeroplanes. The 'civilian' Tigers were now impressed into military service with RAF serial numbers and repainted in the standard RAF training colours of camouflaged brown and green upper surfaces and trainer yellow undersides.

After 12 weeks spent at the EFTS, successful students would now graduate to one of nine Service Flying Training Schools, where they would spend a further 22 weeks graduating from Tiger Moths to more complex service types, at the same time being streamed to single-engined or multi-engined types. Ultimately, two weeks of intensive bombing or gunnery school would take the pilot into the operational environment, 50 weeks after what was likely to have been their first flying experience.

Production continued apace at Hatfield to meet increasing demand from both the RAF and the Royal Navy. The Tiger Moths were also being fitted with added equipment to meet their increased training role.

From the beginning, Tiger Moths had provision for the optional fitment of a 'blind

flying hood' over the rear cockpit. More examples came to be thus fitted as instrument-flying training became a key part of the syllabus.

While the instructor kept a safe lookout from the front cockpit, a canvas, 'pram-hood' could be pulled over the rear cockpit. It obscured all outside vision, forcing the pupil to fly solely by reference to the compass, airspeed indicator, altimeter and a suction gyro-driven Reid and Sigrist turn and slip indicator.

This section of the course was among the least popular, former student Charles Hall describing the hood as a 'totally suffocating, claustrophobic torture-chamber'. Yet the skills learned here would later benefit all trainees, not least those mustered to crew

ABOVE: This Tiger Moth is a unique survivor of the aircraft which carried out the 'scarecrow' anti-submarine patrols around Britain's coastline in 1939 and 1940. *(Stephen Slater)*

LEFT: With instructor in charge and the blind-flying hood raised, a Tiger Moth departs from No 10 EFTS at Yatesbury near Bristol in April 1940. *(deHMC)*

ABOVE: The rear cockpit of this Tiger Moth shows the controls for navigation, signalling and instrument lights on the right cockpit wall. *(BAe via deHMC)*

BELOW: 'Anti-spin' strakes are an identifying feature of the majority of British-built wartime Tiger Moths. *(deHMC)*

bombers on night-time missions over occupied Europe.

As night-flying became an increasingly important part of the training syllabus many Tiger Moths were equipped for nocturnal instruction with the addition of instrument illumination, an identification light under the fuselage capable of flashing in Morse code and navigation lights on the wingtips and tail, powered by a battery located in the front cockpit. No landing light was fitted, although some Tiger Moths had the provision of lighting the final stages of an emergency landing by means of flares fitted on brackets under each wingtip.

Radio equipment was still in its infancy,

relatively speaking, and was deemed too big and heavy for the Tiger Moth. Almost all training flights were therefore conducted on the principle of 'see and avoid', with minimal ground control.

The student flew from the rear cockpit whether solo or with an instructor, as the occupation of the front cockpit, close to the centre of gravity, made little difference to the aircraft's balance. Communication between the two cockpits was via an acoustic device known as the 'Gosport Tube' which worked on a similar principle to a doctor's stethoscope, a mouthpiece being attached by flexible tubes to the earpieces of the other occupant's leather flying helmet. Amazingly this system served almost all wartime students, and was only replaced by an electrical intercom very much later.

The addition of military equipment, plus the fitment of aileron mass balances, strengthened wing spars and layers of paint added during the application of camouflage, created a problem when a number of Tiger Moths proved reluctant to recover from spinning exercises. In September 1941 an urgent investigation at Boscombe Down provided a solution known as 'Mod 112'.

One of the problems, an increasingly rearward centre of gravity, was addressed by the removal of the balance weights from the ailerons, which meant a slight reduction in maximum diving speed. A more visible solution was the fitment of aluminium strakes extending the line of the leading edge of the tailplane alongside the fuselage. These 'anti-spin strakes' are a hallmark of the majority of British wartime-build Tiger Moths today.

The Tiger grows teeth

Not only was the de Havilland Tiger Moth a mainstay of RAF training, it briefly played a more active role. In late 1939 and early 1940, Tiger Moths operated by pilots of No 81 Squadron provided a much-needed liaison service during the Battle of France and remained operational right up to the evacuation from Dunkirk.

As Britain prepared for a final stand against invasion, one of the less orthodox weapons to be considered was the 'Para-slasher'. It was invented by a WW1 veteran, Squadron Leader George Reid, and was tested by Squadron Leader George Lowdell, Commanding Officer of 7EFTS at Desford in Leicestershire.

Effectively a farmer's scythe on an 8ft (2.4m) pole, it was designed to hinge down below the Tiger Moth's fuselage and cut through a descending paratrooper's canopy, or to harry forces on the ground. In the hands of Lowdell, an acknowledged pre-war 'crazy flying' expert, the Paraslasher proved surprisingly effective.

A more sinister proposal was to turn Tiger Moths into what J.M. Bruce of the RAF Museum describes as 'human crop sprayers'. They would have used powder dispensers located under the wings and a tank fitted in the front cockpit filled with 'Paris Green' – an extremely poisonous insecticide – to 'dust' invading troops.

A more conventional form of armament was proposed by de Havilland, who produced 1,500 sets of bomb racks. Carrying up to eight 20lb or 25lb bombs, the Tiger Moths were to be flown solo and the pilots – instructors from the flying schools – would aim their bombs using the cross-wires between the centre-section struts. Of course, should such flights have been necessary in anger they would have presented an almost suicidal scenario of slow-moving aircraft attacking well-equipped ground forces.

However, there was a lighter side too. The instructors were given the freedom to practice low-level bombing techniques and it became a heaven-sent opportunity to break the monotonous routine of training. For a brief period Tiger Moths were 'hedge-hopping' between woods, along rivers and returning to base trailing so many telegraph wires from their undercarriage that the GPO complained that it was being hard-pressed to maintain telephone communications in some areas of the country.

A further active role was the creation of five Coastal Patrol Flights, which were established with Tiger Moths and impressed Hornet Moths to patrol for U-boats around the coastline. The aircraft, based at Dyce near Aberdeen, Abbotsinch on the Clyde, Hooton near Chester, Aldergrove in Northern Ireland and Tenby in South Wales, patrolled in all weathers through the winter of 1939–40 before being replaced by more suitable twin-engined types.

They carried no depth charges, no radio and not even a life raft. A basket in the front cockpit carried two carrier pigeons, which were to be released should the aircraft be ditched. Yet despite the crudity of the equipment these

'Scarecrow' flights played a vital role, as the mere sight or sound of any aircraft was deemed sufficient to keep a U-boat and its periscope below the surface.

ABOVE: Bomb racks were fitted to Tiger Moths in 1940 as a last-ditch anti-invasion measure. *(deHMC)*

Mass production

A further significant move was to affect the production of Tiger Moth aircraft in 1940. De Havilland had secretly been developing a high-speed, all-wood light bomber, which was now receiving significant official attention. This masterpiece was, of course, the Mosquito, and de Havilland was instructed to turn over the entire resources of the Hatfield factory to its production.

Tiger Moth production was therefore transferred from Hatfield to the Morris Motors factory at Cowley in the city of Oxford. This car-making company, of course, had no prior experience of building aircraft, and in addition had lost many skilled workers to the armed forces, yet its ability to switch to building Tiger Moths was a triumph of wartime versatility.

Not only did Morris Motors meet aircraft construction standards, they also added their expertise in flow-line production techniques and pioneered jig-welding of the tubular steel fuselages to boost production rates. While a little over 2,000 Tiger Moths and variants had been built at Hatfield since 1933, more than 3,500 were built between April 1940 and 15 August 1945, when the last Tiger Moth was completed at Cowley.

4 Moulded wooden top decking and fabric covering are applied.

5 Cabane struts and the tail units are fitted to complete fuselage assembly.

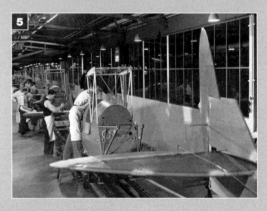

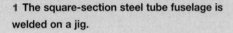

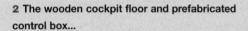

1 The square-section steel tube fuselage is welded on a jig.

2 The wooden cockpit floor and prefabricated control box...

3 ... are bolted into position.

6 The wooden control box, bolted to the cockpit floor, contains all control linkages.

7 Final fuselage assembly includes fitting of fuel tank and engine mounts.

8 With undercarriage fitted, the fitment of engine controls takes place.

9 In the paint shop, camouflage and national markings are applied.

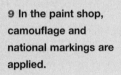

10 Wing rib assembly used many small components to minimise off-cuts.

11 The ribs, positioned on the spars, give the wing its profile

12 Linen fabric is glued, stitched, then 'doped' to create a strong, light structure.

13 Final inspection includes 'truing' the airframe by adjusting the rigging wires.

ABOVE: A Tiger Moth in Rhodesia in 1943, guarded by members of the Air Askari Corps. *(deHMC)*

Spreading wings worldwide

Yet more Tiger Moths were demanded for use around the world. Pre-war RAF expansion plans had identified a need for 50,000 aircrew annually, but even at their peak the training programmes in Britain could only supply 22,000. To overcome this shortfall, in December 1939 the British government proposed that the governments of Commonwealth countries jointly establish a pool of trained aircrew who could then serve with the RAF. The scheme became known as the British Commonwealth Air Training Plan.

In addition to the pilots of Australia, Canada, India, New Zealand, Rhodesia and South Africa who were trained under the scheme, they were joined by many British pilots who were posted overseas to allow instruction to proceed in less

crowded and less hostile skies. Tiger Moths became the main equipment of 25 Flying Schools in Canada, 12 in Australia, seven in South Africa, five in Rhodesia and two in India, training not just pilots but other flight crews such as radio operators too.

While de Havilland overseas factories had previously produced Moths and Tiger Moths in pre-war years, the scale of overseas manufacture now multiplied. At least 345 are recorded to have been built at de Havilland's facility in Auckland, New Zealand, and sets of components were shipped for assembly in Bombay, India. A total of over 1,000 Tiger Moths were built in Australia at Bankstown in New South Wales, many powered by Gipsy Major engines built locally by Holden Motors.

The largest overseas producer of Tiger Moths was de Havilland Canada, who built over 1,700 aircraft between August 1939 and the end of 1942. While there were inevitably local variations in the manufacture of all Tiger Moths, the Canadian-built aeroplanes carried more significant changes to allow them to operate in more extreme North American weather conditions.

They were sufficiently different to be redesignated DH82c. The most obvious change was the incorporation of a larger forward windscreen and enclosed cockpit canopy, which, along with a longer exhaust incorporating a cabin heater, allowed more comfortable winter operation.

Less obvious changes included the

RIGHT: Many of the Tiger Moths built at Bankstown in New South Wales, Australia, were powered by locally-built Gipsy Major engines from Holden Motors. *(deHMC)*

an '82A showing some canadian additions
walkway
oil tank winter cover
coupe top
padded instrument panels
blind flying curtain — folded down on other side
Was raised on a track running closely with the canopy frame

replacement of wooden interplane struts by streamlined-section tubular steel. The undercarriage was swept slightly further forward to minimise the risk of nosing over, as brakes were now fitted to the main-wheels and a tail-wheel was fitted in replacement of the steerable tailskid. Other refinements included a two-piece engine cowling, bigger oil tank and aerodynamic trim tabs fitted to the elevators instead of the previous spring-bias device.

A boost to DH82c climb performance was given by the fitment of Gipsy Major 1C engines to most aircraft, which developed 145hp – around 15hp more than those fitted to other Tiger Moths. When in 1940–41, however, the shipment of Gipsy Major engines from Britain was threatened by shipping losses to German U-boats, 136 Tiger Moths were produced with 120hp Menasco Pirate engines sourced from the USA. Their relative lack of power made them unpopular, and many were subsequently scrapped or refitted with Gipsy engines later in their lives.

Peacetime, retirement, work...and play

By the end of 1944 the requirement for flight training was already reducing, and in August 1945 the last of the 8,800 Tiger Moths to be produced were already surplus to requirements. In post-war Britain the Tiger Moth continued to play a role, however, as a cost-effective means

by which wartime pilots could retain their skills as members of the Royal Air Force Volunteer Reserve.

By 1947 many of the Elementary Flying Training Schools had been regrouped to form 22 Reserve Flying Schools around the country. They and 18 University Air Squadrons each received refurbished Tiger Moths resplendent in new paint schemes which were a far cry from wartime camouflage.

At first aeroplanes appeared in bright overall Trainer Yellow, then in a new post-war livery of silver with yellow bands around fuselages and wings. In contrast to the atmosphere of austerity which surrounded civilian life in post-war Britain, the members of the RAFVR briefly enjoyed an existence described as the 'best flying club' in Britain. They even had the added benefit of being paid for their flying!

Meanwhile, surplus Tiger Moths were now being sold off by the Air Ministry to civilian owners at around £50 for an airworthy example. New engines, still in their packing cases, cost a mere £5, while some highly utilised aeroplanes in a poor state of repair were sold for as little as £20.

One owner spoke of acquiring just such a Tiger Moth, to find that its tank was still full of fuel. This was allegedly then sold off, recouping much of the asking price.

Another Tiger Moth is recorded as having cost its 'owner' even less. Members of a Royal Navy fighter squadron on the aircraft carrier HMS *Pursuer* had discovered, during operations

RAFVR and University Air Squadron Tiger Moths in silver and yellow livery were a familiar sight over the UK in the late 1940s and early 1950s. *(deHMC)*

in the Far East in 1945, a brand new Tiger Moth which had been stored in the packing cases in which it had been shipped from Australia just before the Japanese invasion. The aeroplane was duly 'embarked' and worked on by members of the squadron during the sea voyage back to the UK.

Just before the ship arrived in the River Clyde the Tiger Moth was flown from the carrier deck and disappeared into Scotland. As far as the authorities are concerned it never existed. It was certainly never (officially) seen again.

Most Tiger Moths arrived in civilian service by more conventional routes, being overhauled and offered with new engines and fabric covering for £500–£600. The first to be 'demobbed' was an early pre-war example, G-ACDG, which had spent the first six years of its life with the de Havilland Flying School at Hatfield.

During its wartime service it had been rebuilt no less than three times after various incidents, and it was rebuilt a fourth time before being sold to Marshalls Flying School at Cambridge on 21 December 1945. In January 1946 this aeroplane became the first to provide a post-war civilian flying lesson and became the precursor of Tiger Moths which were operated by flying clubs, air taxi services, flying schools and other aviation businesses around the world.

After a year at Cambridge, G-ACDG was sold to the Netherlands, where, in common with Belgium and France, Tiger Moths formed a new nucleus for flying training, as almost all pre-war light aircraft had been destroyed during the German occupation. Some 40 Tiger Moths were registered in Belgium alone, while in Paris Viscount Yves le Gallais acquired over 100 aeroplanes to be sold among French flying clubs.

As the last RAF Volunteer Reserve Tiger Moths were replaced by more modern DHC-1 Chipmunk and Percival Prentice aircraft in the early 1950s, the flow of surplus aircraft became a flood. One of the largest operations to convert the aircraft to meet the demands of the civil authorities was Rollason Aircraft and Engines, who at their peak had almost 200 Tiger Moths parked at Croydon aerodrome in Surrey.

Many of these overhauled Tiger Moths were delivered to the flying clubs and flying groups which were formed to cater for a new generation of RAF-trained, but now civilian pilots. Others

continued to introduce new recruits to club flying or earned their keep towing sailplanes for the rapidly growing gliding movement. The Tiger Moth also played a formative role in a new industry, agricultural aviation.

While 'crop dusting' had been used in the USA for a number of years, it wasn't until the late 1950s that farmers in other parts of the world were able to reap the benefits of spraying from aircraft. In Britain, Africa, Australia and New Zealand the ready availability, low cost and reliability of the Tiger Moth made it economically viable to treat large areas with fertiliser or pesticides for the first time.

Most Tiger Moth crop-sprayers were fitted with a dry powder hopper in the front cockpit, with the chemicals being discharged through a vent under the fuselage. Later, Tiger Moths were developed to spray liquid fertilisers using a wind-driven pump and spray bars mounted under the lower wings, or using a rotary atomiser to generate a fine mist behind the aeroplane.

Contrary to popular belief, crop-spraying pilots didn't normally carry out low-level stall

LEFT: G-ALWW, known as 'Weary Willie', spent a number of years as a club trainer, then became a glider tug. Its instrument panel contains a number of extra instruments including a cylinder head temperature gauge to the right of the compass, and a gliding variometer on the top left of the panel to show rising or sinking air conditions. The large yellow knob is the emergency quick-release handle for the towline. (Geoff Collins)

BELOW: The Rollasons Aircraft hangar at Croydon was the prime location in Britain for storing and recommissioning war-surplus Tiger Moths. (deHMC)

RIGHT: In the late 1950s former Fleet Air Arm pilot Bill Bowker established Farm Aviation, first at Luton Airport and subsequently at Rush Green in Bedfordshire. He and his fleet of adapted Tiger Moths were pioneers in introducing agricultural aviation into the UK. *(deHMC)*

turns at the end of each run. Bill Bowker, who operated Tiger Moths from 1958 until they were replaced by purpose-built American types in the late 1960s, advocated a tight 'racetrack' pattern around the field, as being less obtrusive and less risky than a U-turn at the each end of the run.

The term 'risky' was relative. An optimum spraying height of less than 10ft (3m), in all weather conditions, taking off and landing 20 times a day from confined fields, meant that many Tiger Moths were lost in crop-spraying service. Other airframes were later to succumb to the corrosive effects of the chemicals used.

The Rollason company remained a prime source of Tiger Moth aircraft and components for more than two decades, operating first from Croydon and then, after the airport's

Naval adventures

The last Tiger Moths to enter British military service were delivered to the Royal Navy. XL714 was operated well into the 1960s from Roborough, attached to the Britannia Flight of Royal Naval College, Dartmouth. It was from here, in June 1964, that the aeroplane made a little Naval history.

At the time, the aircraft carrier HMS *Eagle* was 'working up' following an extensive refit at Devonport and it was deemed that the deck handling crews needed practical handling experience before accommodating the rather heavier fast jets and helicopters. Thus one of the Tiger Moth's last sorties before retirement from the Navy saw a flight of four from Roborough making contact with the carrier in the Western Channel and landing without difficulty on the huge deck.

As the deck crews 'struck down' the Tiger Moths by lift into the echoing hangar decks below for overnight storage, the flight crews were described as 'appraising the wardroom facilities'. They were probably justified in celebrating the last ever biplane flights to and from an aircraft carrier.

Royal Navy Tiger Moths made history in 1964 as the last biplanes to operate from an aircraft carrier, during the 'working up' of *HMS Eagle*. *(deHMC)*

closure, from Redhill and Fairoaks in Surrey. The company's owner Norman Jones was also a keen sporting pilot and in 1956 created one of the most unusual flying clubs ever.

Norman and a group of like-minded enthusiasts mooted the idea of a club for Tiger Moth-type aircraft, and more particularly their carefree style of flying, which in their view was being continually undermined by the need for radios, air traffic control and regulation. The club was unique in not offering any flying training. To qualify one had to have a minimum of 100 flying hours in charge of an aeroplane and pass a flight test in a Tiger Moth.

Jones contributed a number of Tiger Moths and other 'interesting' aeroplanes from Rollason's inventory and found an enthusiastic Honorary Chief Flying Instructor in C. Nepean Bishop, a former RAF instructor. 'Bish' advocated the highest standards of airmanship, actively encouraging formation flying, air racing and aerobatics.

Thus was formed the Tiger Club. Initially based at Croydon, then at Redhill in Surrey, in 1990 it moved to Headcorn in Kent, where it continues today to offer a unique atmosphere and fleet of aircraft to its members.

In addition to promoting airmanship, the Tiger Club and a spin-off organisation known as 'The Barnstormers' also did a great deal to promote flying for fun, touring Britain with small air shows during the 1960s.

These air shows undoubtedly aided the future survival of the Tiger Moth breed. They reawakened a feeling of public nostalgia for a return to the delights of open-cockpit flying.

The 1970s saw the start of renovation of once-discarded airframes and engines – in barns, hangars, sheds and even in a few eccentrics' living rooms. One was even restored in an apartment in a Manhattan skyscraper!

As these restoration projects have borne fruit and more Tiger Moths have returned to the air in recent decades, a new generation of pilots and engineers have committed themselves to learning the skills required to keep the aeroplanes alive.

Today every Tiger Moth is carefully cherished, yet only a small proportion are merely static museum-pieces. A Tiger Moth's natural element is in the air and, thanks to a legion of enthusiasts, it will remain so for decades to come.

OPPOSITE: G-ADIA was originally delivered to the de Havilland School of Flying at Hatfield in 1935. Pressed into wartime service, it was operated by the Fleet Air Arm for air experience flights into the 1960s. Now fully restored, it again carries its original pre-war colours.
(Geoff Collins)

LEFT: The deHMC logo is based on the original badge used by de Havilland on DH60 Moth aeroplanes in the 1920s. *(deHMC)*

BELOW: The original de Havilland standard from the Hatfield factory is traditionally flown at key de Havilland Moth Club events. *(Stephen Slater)*

The de Havilland Moth Club

While owners' clubs for classic cars are not too unusual, the smaller numbers of survivors normally means that the creation of a dedicated marque club for vintage aeroplanes is less viable. One significant exception to this rule is the de Havilland Moth Club.

The Club was first created in 1975, the brainchild of Stuart McKay, who at the time had newly acquired a derelict Tiger Moth from southern France and had embarked on its restoration. Today it has a membership of over 3,000, who own, fly or are enthusiasts of de Havilland aeroplanes, ranging from the original DH60 Moth through the Tiger Moth and its variants to the twin-engined Dragons, Dragonflies and Dragon Rapides.

Stuart, who had learned to fly in 1963 and subsequently constructed a Jodel home-built single-seater, acquired his aeroplane in 1972. It could probably, after a little work, have been reassembled and flown, but it was to remain earthbound for many years, as, due to its influence, Stuart's life headed off in a new direction.

In August 1975 he circulated a letter to about 100 registered owners of British-based Tiger Moths, suggesting that they might form a Tiger Moth Owner's Circle (TMOC).

'The aim was to provide information on spares wanted and available, general chit-chat, and perhaps organise an event or two. I recognised that 1975 was the 50th anniversary of the first DH60 Moth, and that celebrations had already been organised in Australia and even the USA, but precisely nothing was planned in the land where the aeroplane had been conceived and born.'

Stuart suggested that anybody sending a donation of £1 to cover postal expenses before 22 February – the symbolic date of the DH60's maiden flight – would be considered a Founder Member. In the event exactly 60 people did, which was regarded by Stuart as a very good sign.

'Then there was the uncanny case of the two telephone calls,' says Stuart. 'The first was from a fellow overhauler. He told me he was desperate to find a windscreen. Within the hour another caller quizzed me on the proposed organisation and casually remarked that he had

an old Tiger Moth windscreen, if ever anybody wanted one!'

The initial intention was that the TMOC would limit membership to owners of a finite number of Tiger Moths. However, one of the earliest respondents was the owner of a Hornet Moth, followed by enquiries from former owners and pilots, past and present engineers, one-time de Havilland employees and pure enthusiasts.

That meant urgent consideration had to be given to establishing a new and more representative name. The most obvious title that appeared to satisfy all departments was the 'de Havilland Moth Club'.

Stuart, a former editor of the magazine *Popular Flying*, quickly got to work on producing photocopied newsletters, distributed on a monthly basis. In June 1976, the eighth issue advised members of the Club's first rally, to be held at the grass airstrip of Little Gransden in Bedfordshire on 22 August.

'The crews of ten Tiger Moths, a Jackaroo, four Hornet Moths, a Puss Moth, Dragon Rapide and 11 other non-Moths arrived, sat, took tea, conversed with one another and eventually went home again,' says Stuart. 'By the end of the day, membership had risen to 134, and names from the USA, Canada, Kenya, Switzerland, New Zealand and Sweden had appeared on the register.'

Stuart also advocated the Club entering into the niche parts supply business, co-ordinating

bulk manufacture of otherwise obsolete components and selling them as a service to members at discount rates. Over the intervening years this facility has proved to be essential in keeping the aeroplanes flying.

Of all deHMC's organised activities, the Woburn Abbey Moth Rally is perhaps the best known. Wishing to revive the airstrip in the deer park once used for her Moths by his great grandmother Mary, Duchess of Bedford, the late Lord Tavistock, Duke of Bedford, asked the Aviation Department of Shell if they could recommend any suitable group to stage a 'fly-in' event. Shell had been a major supporter of the Famous Grouse Rally only the year before, and unhesitatingly suggested the de Havilland Moth Club.

The first 'Woburn' took place in August 1980, when 28 Moths arrived. It was intended to be a one-off meeting, but the Tavistock family invited the Club back for a second year. As encouragement, Lady Tavistock donated a substantial silver cup to be known as the 'Flying Duchess Trophy' for annual presentation to the best-presented aeroplane. It remains the Club's premier award.

The Woburn event continued until 2007, when changes in estate management policies precluded its running. For 2008, emphasis switched to a charity flying event and air display in association with an 'At Home' day at RAF Halton in Buckinghamshire.

ABOVE: In 2008 the deHMC combined a charity flying event with an air show and open day at RAF Halton in Buckinghamshire. It recreated much of the garden-party atmosphere of the Woburn events.
(Geoff Collins)

In addition to over 50 Moths, other vintage types which took part in the event included a Spitfire, Hurricane and DC-3, and there were also the massed jets of the Queen's Birthday RAF flypast. As a final accolade the event was again graced by the presence of Henrietta, Dowager Duchess of Bedford, the Club's Honorary President.

Another key event in the Club's calendar is the annual 'Moth Forum', which over a period of three days allows participating members to attend lectures by experts in their field. They cover every subject, from buying a Moth to becoming a proficient formation pilot in one, along with every aspect of inspection, maintenance, repair and operation.

These activities are supported by a highly popular illustrated magazine, appropriately called *The Moth*. An intermediate news update service, *Moth Minor*, is published about eight times a year, while an 'Electric Moth' is circulated regularly to those with e-mail access. The Club has further embraced the electronic media revolution by establishing a website at www.dhmothclub.co.uk.

Yet perhaps the most important contribution that the Club has made in ensuring the future of the Tiger Moth is by its continuing provision of design support for the type. Without suitable design authority, modern airworthiness legislation would otherwise have severely curtailed the Tiger Moth's use, or even, in some countries, grounded the aircraft type completely.

Until the late 1990s this responsibility remained vested in British Aerospace, who had inherited it from Hawker Siddeley, who had in turn acquired the responsibility when they took over de Havilland in 1959. British Aerospace, while experienced in engineering modern airliners, missiles and combat aircraft, freely admitted their skills didn't always extend to vintage biplanes!

The deHMC Technical Support Group (TSG) was therefore formed using the wealth of experience within the club. It at first provided an additional source of technical expertise to BAE Systems (the new name for British Aerospace), and subsequently contributed to the creation of a new independent company, de Havilland Support Ltd (DHSL), which now handles all engineering support for the classic de Havilland types.

As for Stuart McKay, his dream of seeing his own Tiger Moth fly was fulfilled when G-AZZZ finally took to the air again in 1998. A year earlier, Stuart was appointed an MBE by Her Majesty the Queen, for services to the de Havilland Moth Club. It was an appropriate accolade, and today, thanks to the continued enthusiasm and efforts of its founder and Secretary, the deHMC continues to go from strength to strength.

Sir Geoffrey de Havilland

The founder of the de Havilland Aircraft Company and the man responsible for the creation of the Tiger Moth, Geoffrey de Havilland can justifiably claim his place as one of aviation's pioneers. His life and career also spanned almost every generation of flight.

Although he retired from active involvement in the company in 1955, after having kept flying until his 70th year, de Havilland continued to visit the factory at Hatfield until his death in 1965. Right up until the end, he continued to

BELOW: Stuart McKay's own Tiger Moth is, of course, a regular attendee at deHMC events, often displayed by former de Havilland and BAe test pilot Desmond Penrose. *(Geoff Collins)*

impress the company's designers with his depth of knowledge of de Havilland projects, including rocket propulsion, the Trident jet airliner and the DH125 business jet, of which he was an enthusiastic advocate.

He was born on 27 July 1882, the second of the three sons and two daughters of Charles de Havilland, the curate of the village of Hazlemere near High Wycombe, Buckinghamshire. After his father gained his own parish in Nuneaton, Warwickshire, the family enjoyed a rural upbringing, first in the Midlands, then at Crux Easton in Hampshire, but Geoffrey and his elder brother Ivon were already interested in all things mechanical. By the time Geoffrey was 14 he had supervised the installation of a generator to provide electricity for the rectory.

Like his father before him, it had been expected that Geoffrey would train for the clergy. Instead, in 1900 he began training at the Crystal Palace Engineering School in London, before moving to an apprenticeship at Willans & Robinson, an engine-maker in Rugby.

Geoffrey then became a draughtsman at the car-maker Wolseley, but, perhaps prompted by the premature death of his elder brother from influenza in 1905, he decided to set out on his own. He began by designing buses for the Motor Omnibus Construction Company in Walthamstow, London. While there he met a young engineer from Cornwall named Frank Hearle. It was the start of a lifelong friendship that would see Hearle become de Havilland's loyal lieutenant in his early flying adventures, works manager of the Hatfield factory, and his brother in law, after marrying Geoffrey's younger sister Ione.

De Havilland and Hearle decided that the future lay in aviation. In 1908, Geoffrey began to design his own aeroplane and persuaded his grandfather to loan him money to finance the project. Believing that there was no suitable engine he designed that too, and had it built for him by the Iris car company in North London. With its air-cooled flat-four configuration, it anticipated modern light aircraft engines.

The structure of the aircraft was inspired by Wright Brothers' and French Farman designs and was literally hand-built by de Havilland and Hearle. Much of the fabric covering was

My De Havilland,

MAYS. Aldershot. 20.

stitched by Geoffrey's wife Louise on a hand-turned Singer sewing machine, which she continued to use for the rest of her life.

In November 1909 the completed aircraft was shipped to a flying field that de Havilland had selected at Seven Barrows, near Newbury. After weeks of attempts Geoffrey eventually forced the aeroplane into the air, only for it to stall and crash. He escaped with bruises, but the aircraft was a write-off; only the engine was salvageable.

He and Hearle returned to their workshop in Fulham and, undaunted, tried again. Happily their second design was more successful, making the first of its many flights on 10 September 1910.

By now, however, their money was running out and both de Havilland and Hearle needed jobs. Geoffrey approached Mervyn O'Gorman, Superintendent of the Balloon Factory at Farnborough, with a view to selling his aeroplane to the Army. The War Office agreed to its purchase and to employ de Havilland as aeroplane designer and test pilot, with Hearle as his mechanic. Shortly afterwards the factory was renamed the Royal Aircraft Factory.

De Havilland was responsible for two important designs in the years preceding World War One. The first was the FE2 (FE standing for 'Farman Experimental'), which was a 'pusher' biplane with the engine behind the pilot. The second was called the BE or 'Bleriot Experimental', to circumvent an arcane rule that prevented the factory designing all-new aeroplanes.

The BE1, which first flew on 27 December 1911, had nothing other than its name in common with the French monoplane on which it was officially based. It was a tractor biplane, with the engine mounted ahead of two seats in tandem, a layout which would continue to the Tiger Moth. By the time the prototype was handed over to the Air Battalion of the Royal Engineers in March 1912, it had made many flights with passengers, been equipped with wireless, and had even flown at night.

The BE2 which succeeded it was effectively the first-ever purpose-designed military aeroplane. Designed with artillery observation in mind, it was the first aeroplane to successfully offer 'hands-off' flying stability. Over 4,000 examples were built between 1912 and 1917, and they served in every major campaign of World War One.

By 1914, however the bureaucracy of the Royal Aircraft Factory was frustrating de Havilland. He resigned after being moved to the Aeronautical Inspection Department, as he wanted to continue to create new aeroplanes, not merely evaluate other peoples' designs.

His skills led to him being quickly snapped up by George Holt Thomas, who had created the Aircraft Manufacturing Company, or Airco, at Hendon. Among his many designs for them, the DH4 and DH9 aircraft were two of the most successful light bombers of the period, being as fast as many contemporary fighters. The DH6, meanwhile, was a simple, cheap and easy-to-build basic trainer. Although larger than

BELOW: The BE2 design, which first flew in 1912, was the start of a line which would lead to the Tiger Moth. *(deHMC)*

the Moth and Tiger Moth designs which would appear a decade later, it used almost the same design principles.

The Armistice in 1918 brought with it the cancellation of production contracts throughout the aircraft industry. Geoffrey therefore turned to civil aviation and, financed by an investment of £10,000 from his former employer George Holt Thomas, along with £3,000 of his personal savings and £1,000 from other sources, on 25 September 1920 he created the de Havilland Aircraft Company, and leased the former London & Provincial Aviation Company site at Stag Lane, Edgware, to be his factory and aerodrome.

At that time there was no suitable type of aircraft available for private ownership. However, a year after the company's creation de Havilland was approached by Alan Samuel Butler, who wanted a new aeroplane built for his personal use.

Butler little realised that he was going to be the company's financial saviour. The owners of the aerodrome had just given de Havilland notice to quit, but an initial investment from Butler allowed them to buy the airfield and secure the factory's future. Butler continued to invest in the company and by 1924 was its chairman.

Thus began the story that led to the production of first the Moth, then the Tiger Moth. The 1930s saw the company expand to a new airfield at Hatfield in Hertfordshire, where in addition to light aeroplanes, de Havilland also manufactured over 800 airliners, including the Dragon, Express and Dragon Rapide types. In 1934 the de Havilland Comet racer won the MacRobertson air race from London to Melbourne in a record-breaking time of less than 71 hours.

During World War Two, in addition to the Tiger Moth, de Havilland's biggest contribution was the Mosquito, which was among the fastest and most versatile warplanes of the era. He was knighted for his services in 1944. In the post-war period de Havilland moved into the jet age with the Vampire fighter and the Comet, which in 1949 became the first civilian jet airliner.

Sadly two of de Havilland's three sons, John and Geoffrey junior, were killed in flying accidents. John died in a wartime midair

collision, while Geoffrey was lost flying the DH108 Swallow high-speed research aircraft in 1946. These deaths are said to have contributed to the early passing of de Havilland's first wife Louise. Yet he later found happiness again with his second wife Joan, and his fascination for invention continued undiminished.

It is notable that when, in 1961, at 79 years of age, Sir Geoffrey de Havilland published his memoirs, entitled *Sky Fever*, he devoted the final 15-page chapter to space travel, whereas memories of his pioneering flights extend to just five pages.

Looking forwards was, in de Havilland's view, always more interesting than looking back.

ABOVE: The success of the DH60 Moth series helped secure the company's future. *(deHMC)*

'Beneath its fabric-covered skin, the construction of the Tiger Moth bridges ancient and modern. The wings use wooden construction which harks back to the dawn of flight, while the modular, welded steel-tube fuselage structure is still used in many light aircraft today.'

Chapter Two

Anatomy of the Tiger Moth

Under the skin

Unlike more exotic warbirds, ownership of a Tiger Moth is within the reach of anyone who, under certified supervision, can maintain or restore an example to airworthy condition. Today, the rising value of these aeroplanes, combined with the relative simplicity of the Tiger Moth's airframe and its robust, reliable power unit, makes even a complete restoration a practical and (almost) financially viable proposition.

LEFT: G-ACDC was one of the first DH82A Tiger Moths to be delivered in 1933. Seen here under restoration for its owners, the Tiger Club, it and sister aeroplane G-ACDA were used for much of the detail photography in this book. *(Stephen Slater)*

DE HAVILLAND D.H.82A TIGER MOTH

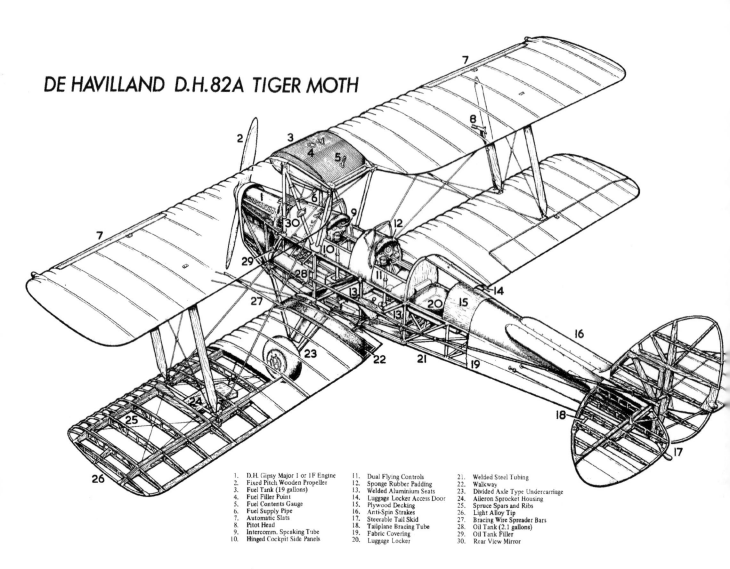

1.	D.H. Gipsy Major 1 or 1F Engine	11.	Dual Flying Controls	21.	Welded Steel Tubing
2.	Fixed Pitch Wooden Propeller	12.	Sponge Rubber Padding	22.	Walkway
3.	Fuel Tank (19 gallons)	13.	Welded Aluminium Seats	23.	Divided Axle Type Undercarriage
4.	Fuel Filler Point	14.	Luggage Locker Access Door	24.	Aileron Sprocket Housing
5.	Fuel Contents Gauge	15.	Plywood Decking	25.	Spruce Spars and Ribs
6.	Fuel Supply Pipe	16.	Anti-Spin Strakes	26.	Light Alloy Tip
7.	Automatic Slats	17.	Steerable Tail Skid	27.	Bracing Wire Spreader Bars
8.	Pitot Head	18.	Tailplane Bracing Tube	28.	Oil Tank (2.1 gallons)
9.	Intercomm. Speaking Tube	19.	Fabric Covering	29.	Oil Tank Filler
10.	Hinged Cockpit Side Panels	20.	Luggage Locker	30.	Rear View Mirror

RIGHT: The fuselage of G-ANDE, stripped to its bare frame, awaits renovation at Sywell.
(Andy Smith)

Theoretically a Tiger Moth can go on forever. The airframe has no finite fatigue life and spare parts remain readily available. However, it is said that operating a Tiger Moth is a continuous process of relearning what others have long forgotten.

In restoration and maintenance terms, to normal engineering skills one needs to add woodworking, sheet metalworking, the mastery of doping linen fabrics, and the intricacies of rigging the aircraft's collection of wings, struts and flying and landing wires. Once these talents have been attained and successfully utilised, the satisfaction of seeing a newly restored Tiger Moth back in the air is unparalleled.

Old meets new

Beneath a fabric-covered skin of cotton or Irish linen, doped with cellulose or butyrate lacquer, the construction of the de Havilland Tiger Moth bridges the gap between ancient and modern. The wings and tail unit use wooden construction which harks back to the pioneering days of flight, yet the modular, welded steel tube fuselage structure is similar in principle to that still used in many modern light aircraft. This easily-repaired, Meccano-style, bolt-together fuselage is a key to the Tiger Moth's longevity.

While there are many minor differences between pre-war and wartime-built aircraft produced at Hatfield and Nuffield, or British-manufactured examples and those constructed around the world during the war years, the basic construction of all remained the same from 1931 to the end of production in 1945. Almost all the parts which fit a 1930s aeroplane will also fit one produced more than a decade later.

At first the Tiger Moth looks crude. Yet there is an elegant and logical simplicity about the design. It is very much 'an engineer's aeroplane'. With the notable exception of the Queen Bee pilotless drone, which used a wooden fuselage to minimise the risk of radio interference, all Tiger Moths used a bolted and welded steel tube fuselage structure with tandem dual cockpits, with the main pilot's seat being in the rear.

The logic of the latter arrangement, carried over from some of the earliest WW1 types, was that the front cockpit was as close as possible to the aircraft's centre of gravity. Whether it was

occupied or not therefore made little difference to the balance. If flown from the front cockpit, with the rear unoccupied, many biplanes of the era require ballast to be carried.

The general control layout and instrumentation of both cockpits was the same, although if required the front cockpit control column could be removed and the rudder bar disconnected. Duplicate throttle controls were provided by extending the linkage from the lever on the left side of the rear cockpit, through the front cockpit to the second set of controls, then on into the engine compartment.

BELOW: The design and construction of the Tiger Moth, with hand-fabricated wooden wings and a bolt-together welded steel-tube fuselage, bridges the gap between ancient and modern. *(British Aerospace/deHMC, from 1944 Maintenance and Repair Manual)*

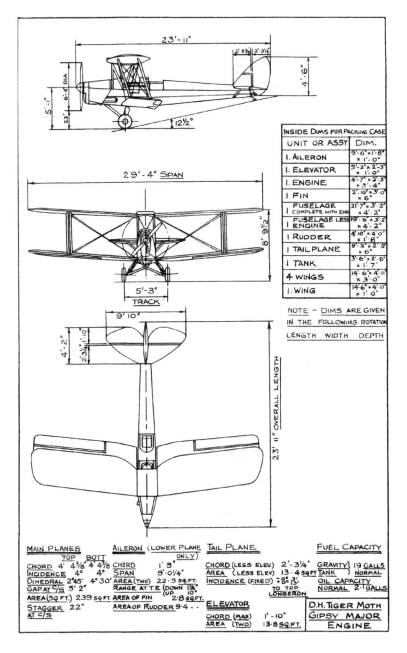

RIGHT: Duplicate
ignition switches
are mounted on
the outside of
each cockpit as an
important safety aid,
allowing the propeller
swinger to confirm
whether the ignition
is 'on' or 'off'. *(Andy Smith)*

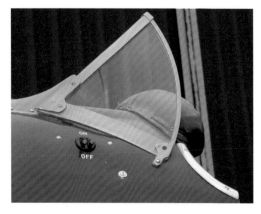

BELOW: Hinged
aluminium engine
cowlings aid access.
The top of the cowling
is reinforced, and with
the aid of a step in
the forward fuselage
gives access to the
top wing-mounted fuel
tank. *(Geoff Collins)*

One distinctive feature of the Tiger Moth is that the duplicate set of ignition switches for the engine's two magnetos are mounted outside the cockpit. This is an important safety aid so that the person swinging the propeller can clearly see whether they are up for 'on' or down for 'off', before handling the propeller for start-up.

Access to the cockpits is aided by hinge-down doors on either side, with a third hatch

to the right of and behind the rear cockpit. This gives access to a baggage compartment, just about large enough to accommodate a small holdall. Today, though, it is more likely to contain a battery (if a radio is fitted), a pair of wheel chocks, a small toolkit, cockpit covers, a litre or two of oil and a supply of rags to clean off the oily residue from the engine after each flight.

The engine itself is housed beneath an aluminium engine cowling which is shaped to provide the optimum air-cooling performance. In the case of British-built Tiger Moths, this is a five-part unit, comprising a nosebowl with an air intake on the port side, two hinged side panels, and top and bottom cowls.

The lower cowling is hinged at the rear to allow access to the bottom of the engine and valve gear, while the upper cowling is reinforced to provide a walkway for access to the upper wing-mounted petrol tank for refuelling. In Canadian-built Tiger Moths the three upper cowling components are replaced by a two-piece cowling with a central hinge.

The mainplanes, each built around a pair of substantial solid or laminated spruce spars, feature ailerons only on the lower wings. In terms of handling this has long been the source of some criticism, as the Tiger Moth's ailerons are relatively ineffective at low airspeeds. However, fitting a single pair of ailerons, as opposed to fitting them on all four wings, means that the control runs are simplified and precious weight can be saved.

There is a further elegant engineering solution built into the aileron controls. Most aeroplanes of the Tiger Moth's era suffer notable 'adverse yaw' due to the greater aerodynamic drag of the downward aileron in the higher pressure airstream on the lower surface of the wing. This causes the nose to swing in the opposite direction from the turn, initiating a side-slip which must be countered with rudder. In the Tiger Moth, however, this tendency is mitigated by differential movement of the ailerons, created by linking the control cables to a sprocket and crank system, linked in turn to the control surfaces by a pushrod.

The full downward movement of one aileron is thus reached before the full upward movement of the other. Then, as the control column continues to be moved to its limit, the

LEFT: This Tiger Moth at the Newark Air Museum displays the structure of the uncovered mainplanes. They are built around a pair of substantial spruce spars, braced with internal wires. *(Stephen Slater with thanks to Newark Air Museum)*

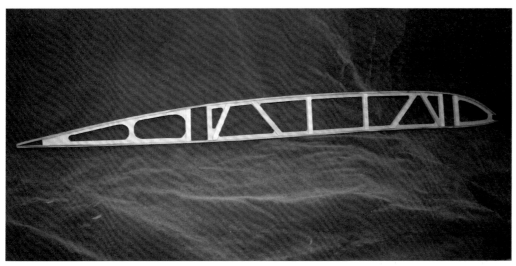

LEFT: The wing ribs, fabricated from small pieces of spruce, give the necessary aerodynamic profile. *(Matt Boddington)*

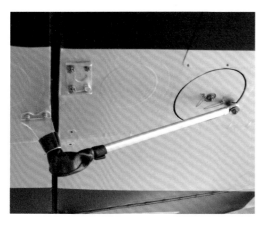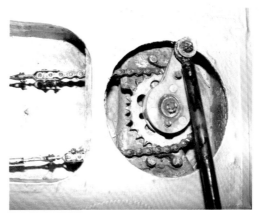

FAR LEFT: An ingenious sprocket and crank system… *(Geoff Collins)*

LEFT: …creates a 'differential aileron' control, minimising adverse yaw when initiating turns. *(Andy Smith)*

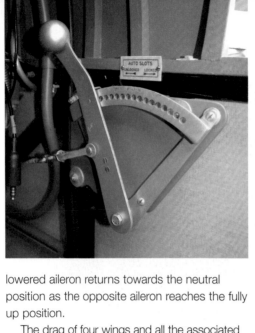

lowered aileron returns towards the neutral position as the opposite aileron reaches the fully up position.

The drag of four wings and all the associated struts and bracing wires means that the Tiger Moth is neither fitted with nor requires landing flaps to reduce its approach speed. Its glide angle is approximately similar to that of a modern Cessna or Piper with their flaps fully deployed.

The upper wings of the majority of Tiger Moths are fitted with a further ingenious device to improve low-speed handling. Aerofoil-shaped slats (or 'slots') on the upper wings are held against the leading edge of the wing by air pressure in normal flight, but at speeds below around 60mph (100kph) they progressively extend by 3in (75mm), encouraging the airflow to remain attached over the top surface of the outer wing, thereby slightly delaying the stall and making it more gentle when it occurs.

The slats – which can be manually locked closed by a control on the right side of the rear cockpit, to avoid sudden deployment during aerobatics or unnecessary wear and tear while taxiing – were developed by another British aircraft designer, Sir Frederick Handley Page. In addition to the cost of the slats and their controls, de Havilland had to pay a royalty of £38 11s 6d on every set fitted, so they were only offered as an extra-cost option on pre-war Tiger Moths. However, all RAF-specification aeroplanes had them fitted.

The correct 'truing' of the aircraft and the rigging of the four wings is a complex and time-consuming exercise involving plumb lines and inclinometers (spirit levels), not to mention several sets of stepladders, as the upper wings of the aeroplane stand some 8ft 9in (2.68m) above the hangar floor. Working outwards from the centre section struts on the fuselage, tolerances of less than half a degree must be adhered to in order to allow the aeroplane to fly safely and without constant control input.

Certification and support

There is a saying in UK aviation that no aeroplane is fit to fly unless the weight of its paperwork is approximately equal to the weight of the airframe. Even with such a relatively simple aeroplane as the Tiger Moth, this maxim apparently holds true.

Unlike many historic aeroplanes, which operate throughout most of Europe under flying restrictions set out on 'permits to fly', the Tiger Moth remains a fully certified aircraft with an internationally recognised Certificate of Airworthiness. This allows its continued operation in revenue-earning activities such as flying instruction, but requires that all but the most basic maintenance tasks are supervised by certified engineers and maintenance organisations.

Many private owners still, legally, work on their own aeroplanes with the approval of licensed engineers, but must operate within specific maintenance schedules and sign-off procedures. At the heart of this arrangement is the work of de Havilland Support Limited (DHSL), who since April 2001 have provided the Design Authority and technical support for the Tiger Moth and many other de Havilland types that ensures their continued operation and airworthiness.

ABOVE: While approved repair schemes cover most scenarios, this one is unlikely to be repeated. In 1941 this Tiger Moth flew through a fireball after 'colliding' with a barrage balloon and, amazingly, managed to return to base for a somewhat shaky landing. It was only after the war that the pilot involved, Bernard Barton, admitted that bored instructors had been passing their time by running their aircrafts' wheels along the tops of the dirigibles! *(deHMC archive)*

OPPOSITE: The main components of the Tiger Moth Gipsy 1 engine. *(deHMC archive)*

National Aviation Authorities of those countries where such aircraft are based.

As a certified aeroplane, any repair must be carried out following a pre-approved repair scheme. Regardless of the quality of work carried out, any failure to do this immediately negates the Certificate of Airworthiness.

DHSL maintains an archive containing a full array of repair drawings and schemes. Thus if an aircraft has damage in excess of published repair schemes, a solution may already be available, or alternatively the company can originate a new repair scheme under the terms of its design approval.

After close to eight decades of service, though, one wonders if there is anything breakable left on a Tiger Moth which has not already been broken and mended at some point in its life!

Engine

General characteristics: Gipsy Major 1

Four-cylinder, normally aspirated, air-cooled inverted in-line piston engine with overhead valves operated by pushrods

Bore:	4.646in (118mm)
Stroke:	5.512in (140mm)
Displacement:	6.124 litres
Length:	48.3in (1,227mm)
Width:	20.0in (508mm)
Height:	29.6in (752mm)
Dry weight:	300lb (136kg) to 322lb (146kg) depending on type
Ignition:	Two BTH AG4 magnetos, each supplying four sparking plugs on each side of the engine
Fuel system:	Downdraught Claudel Hobson AI48 carburettor, gravity-fed from 19-gallon (86-litre) fuel tank in upper wing centre section
Oil system:	Dry sump, with gear-type feed pump and gravity return to an oil tank of 2.1-gallon (9.5-litre) capacity on port side of fuselage
Power output:	122hp (91kW) at 2,100rpm for take-off

DHSL's offices and archives at the Imperial War Museum, Duxford, not only contain all the technical documentation held successively by Hawker Siddeley Aviation, British Aerospace and BAE Systems, who inherited them from de Havilland, but also possess a skilled team of professional engineers. These enable DHSL to be regarded under International Civil Aviation Organisation (ICAO) requirements as a Type Design Organisation with technical responsibility for the DH60 Moth and the DH82A Tiger Moth as well as aircraft such as the DH89A Dragon Rapide, DH104 Dove, DH114 Heron and DHC-1 Chipmunk.

This requires the Company to undertake tasks such as maintaining the accuracy of technical manuals, issuing the equivalent of Service Bulletins and maintenance instructions and responding to enquiries from aircraft owners, maintenance organisations or the

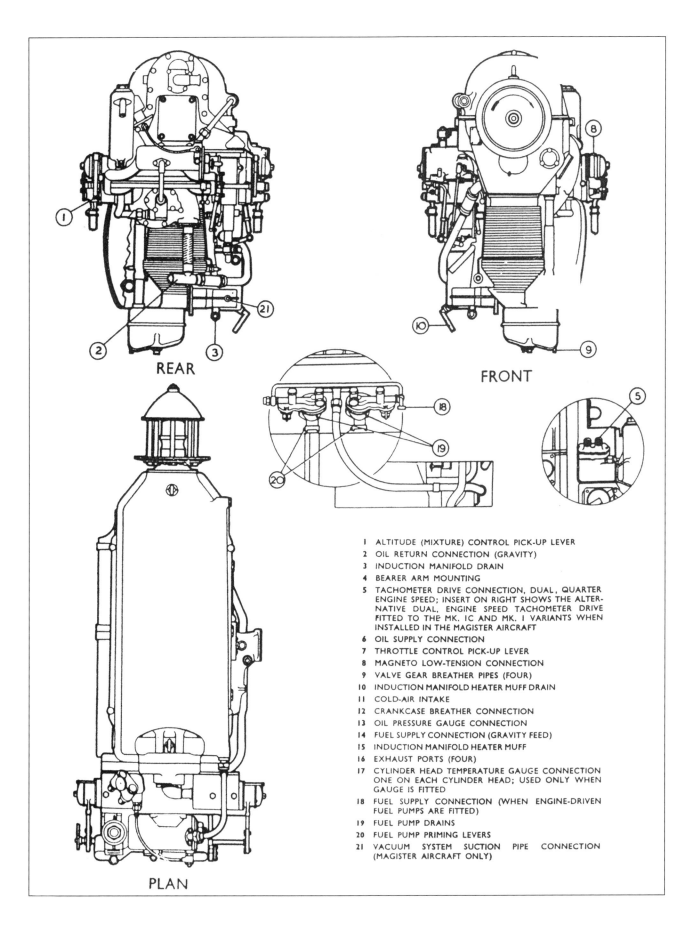

REAR

FRONT

PLAN

1 ALTITUDE (MIXTURE) CONTROL PICK-UP LEVER

2 OIL RETURN CONNECTION (GRAVITY)

3 INDUCTION MANIFOLD DRAIN

4 BEARER ARM MOUNTING

5 TACHOMETER DRIVE CONNECTION, DUAL, QUARTER ENGINE SPEED; INSERT ON RIGHT SHOWS THE ALTERNATIVE DUAL, ENGINE SPEED TACHOMETER DRIVE FITTED TO THE MK. IC AND MK. I VARIANTS WHEN INSTALLED IN THE MAGISTER AIRCRAFT

6 OIL SUPPLY CONNECTION

7 THROTTLE CONTROL PICK-UP LEVER

8 MAGNETO LOW-TENSION CONNECTION

9 VALVE GEAR BREATHER PIPES (FOUR)

10 INDUCTION MANIFOLD HEATER MUFF DRAIN

11 COLD-AIR INTAKE

12 CRANKCASE BREATHER CONNECTION

13 OIL PRESSURE GAUGE CONNECTION

14 FUEL SUPPLY CONNECTION (GRAVITY FEED)

15 INDUCTION MANIFOLD HEATER MUFF

16 EXHAUST PORTS (FOUR)

17 CYLINDER HEAD TEMPERATURE GAUGE CONNECTION ONE ON EACH CYLINDER HEAD; USED ONLY WHEN GAUGE IS FITTED

18 FUEL SUPPLY CONNECTION (WHEN ENGINE-DRIVEN FUEL PUMPS ARE FITTED)

19 FUEL PUMP DRAINS

20 FUEL PUMP PRIMING LEVERS

21 VACUUM SYSTEM SUCTION PIPE CONNECTION (MAGISTER AIRCRAFT ONLY)

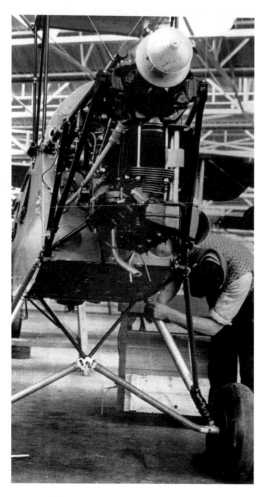

RIGHT: The Gipsy Major engine marked a continuous evolution from the pre-WW1 air-cooled V8 Renault engine, through the upright ADC Cirrus and Gipsy I, to the inverted inline four-cylinder configuration. *(deHMC archive)*

The de Havilland Gipsy Major engine can trace its roots to World War One, via the early air-cooled V-8 engines from Renault and the Royal Aircraft Factory, which provided the cylinder assemblies of the ADC Cirrus engine of the 1920s. However, by the time the first Gipsy Major engine was produced in 1932 de Havilland was already established as Britain's leading builder of light aircraft engines, and the Gipsy engine had earned a reputation for performance, quality and, most important of all, reliability.

While the earlier de Havilland Gipsy engines were of upright design, similar to an automobile engine, with the oil contained in a sump beneath the crankcase, the Gipsy Major is fitted in the Tiger Moth in an inverted configuration, with the cylinders suspended below the crankshaft. This allowed the thrust line and propeller to be kept in a high position without the cylinders blocking the pilot's forward view, gave better propeller clearance, and placed the exhaust pipe well below cockpit level.

One disadvantage of the configuration is that it required the engine's piston rings and gaskets to be maintained in tip-top condition to minimise oil consumption and leaks. Of course, age and the hard work endured by most Gipsy Major engines work against their remaining totally oil-tight,

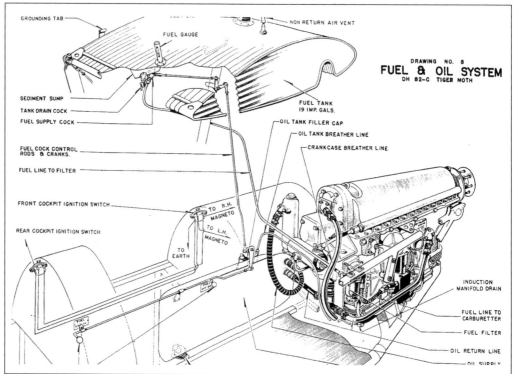

DRAWING NO. 8
FUEL & OIL SYSTEM
DH 82-C TIGER MOTH

GROUNDING TAB — NON RETURN AIR VENT — FUEL GAUGE — SEDIMENT SUMP — TANK DRAIN COCK — FUEL SUPPLY COCK — FUEL TANK 19 IMP. GALS. — OIL TANK FILLER CAP — OIL TANK BREATHER LINE — CRANKCASE BREATHER LINE — FUEL COCK CONTROL RODS & CRANKS. — FUEL LINE TO FILTER — FRONT COCKPIT IGNITION SWITCH — TO R.H. MAGNETO — REAR COCKPIT IGNITION SWITCH — TO L.H. MAGNETO — TO EARTH — INDUCTION MANIFOLD DRAIN — FUEL LINE TO CARBURETTER — FUEL FILTER — OIL RETURN LINE — OIL SUPPLY

RIGHT: This image from a contemporary manual shows the 'dry sump' oil system, with a 2.1-gallon (9.5-litre) remote oil tank, and the fuel system. *(deHMC)*

leading to many earning the nicknames 'Dripsy Gipsy' or 'Dripsy Major'!

The 2.1-gallon (9.5-litre) oil tank meant that oil consumption of up to 2 pints (1.1 litres) an hour was not an issue in wartime service, and subsequent modifications to the oil control ring have reduced this level of consumption significantly.

While the relatively straightforward nature of the Gipsy Major allows many organisations around the world to successfully overhaul and maintain these engines, two companies in Great Britain are regarded as centres of excellence for the type.

Deltair Airmotive at Waterlooville in Hampshire are custodians of a Type Responsibility Agreement with the UK Civil Aviation Authority. Among their records are copies of the master manuals, Technical News Sheets and drawings for the entire Gipsy range, as well as lists of the original modifications since the 1930s. The company also maintains a stock of Gipsy parts and provides certified overhauled engines and repair work.

Vintage Engine Technology (Vintech) at Little Gransden in Bedfordshire was established in 1991 by Tiger Moth restorer Mike Vaisey and engineer Paul Sharman, to specialise in the repair and restoration of vintage and out-of-production aero-engines and their accessories. The company now operates under CAA and EASA Approval for the complete restoration of all models of the Gipsy engine and other similar types.

Long production run, many variants

A total of 14,615 Gipsy Major I engines were built by de Havilland between 1932 and 1945. Production also continued post-war, with more than 1,500 examples of the Gipsy Major 10 series being produced for aircraft such as the Auster and the DHC-1 Chipmunk.

Although these later engines share the same bore and stroke, they can have different splined crankshaft noses, additional oil scavenge pumps and various different accessory cases at the back of the engine. It is therefore not possible to install all of them in Tiger Moths without significant modification.

Within the Gipsy Major 1 series there are also a number of type variations, most specifically to withstand the higher octane fuels which were developed during the war years. The

ABOVE: The straightforward nature of the Gipsy Major engine, with four individual cylinder barrels on a common crankcase, leant itself to hand assembly. Now as then, this allows the engine to be stripped, repaired and overhauled to 'as new' condition. *(deHMC)*

BELOW: One of the many changes during the long life of the Gipsy Major engine was the introduction of aluminium alloy heads with separate stainless steel valve seats. These heads (left) have greater finning to disperse heat and are more resilient than the earlier aluminium bronze cylinder heads (right) to attack from the leaded aviation fuels in general use today. *(Geoff Collins)*

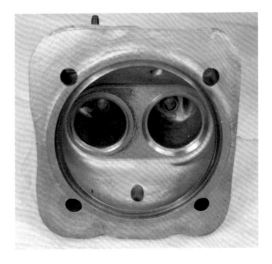

LEFT: This aluminium bronze cylinder head has been overhauled with stainless steel valve seats. However, some signs of earlier pitting from the effects of leaded aviation fuel can still be seen. *(Geoff Collins)*

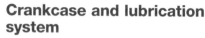

RIGHT: The cast aluminium crankcase forms the foundation of the entire engine. The four individual cylinder barrels are each attached to its lower face via studs. *(Geoff Collins)*

BELOW: The upper half of the crankcase, known as the 'top cover', is a magnesium alloy casting, secured to the lower half by 27 bolts and nuts and eight studs. *(Stephen Slater)*

BELOW RIGHT: The crankshaft runs in five white, metal-lined shell bearings, with thrust loads taken by a separate thrust bearing at the front of the crankcase. *(Geoff Collins)*

original Gipsy Major 1 utilised aluminium bronze cylinder heads, but to enable the use of leaded fuels new aluminium alloy heads with separate stainless steel valve seats were fitted to the Mark 1F and Mark 1C.

While the Mk1F engine maintained the same 5.25:1 compression ratio and 122hp (92kW) maximum output as the original Gipsy Major 1, the Mk1C used pistons with a raised crown. These produced a higher 6:1 compression ratio and a potential maximum take-off power of 143hp (109kW), although this was only achieved with a fine-pitched propeller.

Crankcase and lubrication system

The cast aluminium crankcase forms the rigid foundation for the entire engine, containing and supporting the bearing loads for the crankshaft, camshaft and pushrods. The four identical cylinders, numbered from the front of the engine, are attached to the lower face of the crankcase, and the crankcase rear wall projects below the line of the cylinder-mounting face to provide the front of the casing for the timing gear, magneto, oil pump and tachometer drives.

The crankcase is divided horizontally on the crankshaft centre line to give access to the crankshaft, main bearings and the big-end bearings on the connecting rods. The upper part of the crankcase, known as the 'top cover', is a magnesium alloy casting and is secured to the main crankcase by 27 bolts and nuts, and eight studs around its perimeter. The top cover also contains two lifting eyes for use when slinging the engine.

The crankshaft runs in five main bearings. These are of the replaceable white metal-lined steel shell type, with a ball-type thrust bearing fitted to the crankshaft. The thrust loads are taken by a separate nose cover at the front of the crankshaft. The lower half main bearing shells contain oil ducts and grooves which align with oilways in the crankcase to allow lubrication of the crankshaft journals.

The lubrication system for the engine is of a 'dry sump' type. An engine-driven oil pump lifts oil from the tank on the port side of the forward fuselage, feeds it under pressure through an Auto-klean filter,

LEFT: The crankshaft is hollow, creating an oilway which allows oil to be fed to the big end bearings. *(Geoff Collins)*

LEFT: The nose of this crankshaft has been modified by Vintech in an approved update, to prevent the risk of cracking and fatigue failure. A strengthening sleeve has been place over the area which absorbs the thrust loads, and the section which engages with the propeller boss has been treated with a sulfanuz coating. *(Geoff Collins)*

BELOW: The 'dry-sump' lubrication system relies on an engine-driven oil pump to lift oil from the remote oil tank situated just above the port wing leading edge. *(deHMC)*

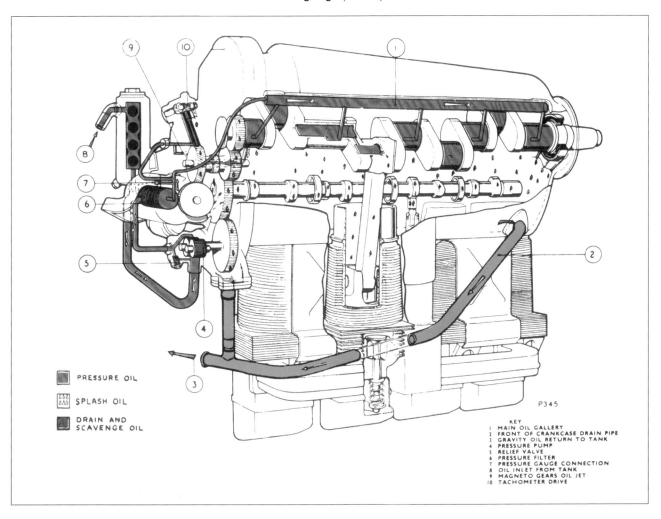

PRESSURE OIL

SPLASH OIL

DRAIN AND SCAVENGE OIL

P345

KEY
1 MAIN OIL GALLERY
2 FRONT OF CRANKCASE DRAIN PIPE
3 GRAVITY OIL RETURN TO TANK
4 PRESSURE PUMP
5 RELIEF VALVE
6 PRESSURE FILTER
7 PRESSURE GAUGE CONNECTION
8 OIL INLET FROM TANK
9 MAGNETO GEARS OIL JET
10 TACHOMETER DRIVE

ABOVE: The oil returns by gravity to the tank. The exposed aluminium face of the tank on the outside of the fuselage also acts as an oil cooler. *(Geoff Collins)*

RIGHT: The ingenious Auto-klean oil filter circulates the lubricating oil… *(Geoff Collins)*

RIGHT: …between close-set, disc-shaped, thin steel plates. *(Geoff Collins)*

FAR RIGHT: The daily rotation of a handle on the outside of the filter allows the discs to rub across scraper blades, cleaning off any sediment. *(Geoff Collins)*

external pipes and an oil gallery on the starboard side of the crankcase top cover, to the main and big-end bearings and ancillary drive gears.

The remaining areas of the engine – the cylinder walls, the five-bearing camshaft and connecting rod little-end bearings – are splash-lubricated as the oil drains downwards through it. Oil pressure is normally maintained at 40 to 45psi (2.81 to 3.16 bar), with a minimum allowable pressure of 35psi (2.46 bar).

On Gipsy Major 1 series engines, the oil returns by gravity to the oil tank through pipes from the front and rear of the engine. The exposed aluminium face of the oil tank in the airflow on the outside of the fuselage acts as a sufficiently effective oil cooler. Some later Gipsy Major variants use scavenge pumps to ensure more efficient lubrication in all attitudes of flight, but these are not normally fitted to Tiger Moths.

The Auto-klean filter is located at the rear of the engine. Inside the filter, the oil percolates between close-set, disc-shaped, thin steel plates set on a central rod. Turning a small handle on the outside of the filter allows these discs to be rotated against a system of scraper blades, allowing the cleaning of any sediment from between the blades. Turning this handle at least a full turn to clean the elements is part of the pre-flight routine before the first flight of the day.

Cylinder barrels, pistons, cylinder heads and valve gear

The four cylinder barrels are identical, machined from carbon steel forgings, and feature cooling fins around their exterior to aid heat dissipation. A short spigot at the upper end of each cylinder slides into the crankcase as far as a machined collar. This additionally acts as an oil dam to prevent oil flooding the cylinder.

Four high tensile steel holding-down studs

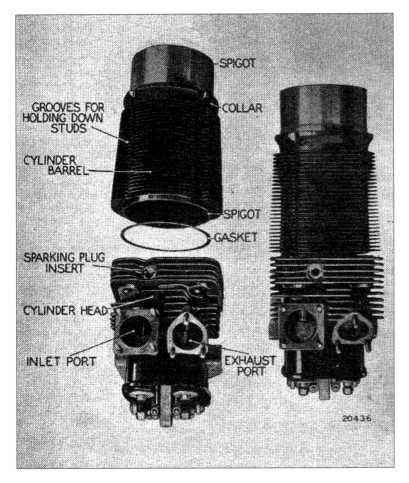

SPIGOT

GROOVES FOR
HOLDING DOWN
STUDS

COLLAR

CYLINDER
BARREL

SPIGOT

GASKET

SPARKING PLUG
INSERT

CYLINDER HEAD

INLET PORT

EXHAUST
PORT

20436

LEFT: Each of the four forged carbon steel cylinder barrels... *(deHMC)*

ABOVE: ...is finned to aid cooling... *(Geoff Collins)*

BELOW: ...and is secured to the crankcase by high tensile steel holding-down studs, which also act as the cylinder head bolts. *(Stephen Slater)*

are screwed into the crankcase at one end and act as the cylinder head bolts at the other, to hold the barrels in position. An O-ring seal and the collar on each cylinder barrel prevent oil leaks and a copper-asbestos or solid copper cylinder head gasket ensures a gas-tight seal.

The pistons and connecting rods within the cylinders underwent a process of steady evolution. The early slipper-type, flat-crowned pistons in Gipsy Major Mk1 and Mk1F engines are machined from heat-treated aluminium alloy castings. The later Mk1C pistons have a higher piston crown to provide greater compression and are made from alloy forgings. These pistons are also strengthened to withstand the increased operating loads in the region of the gudgeon pin which attaches the piston to the forged I-section connecting rod.

Each piston carries three rings of rectangular section situated in grooves between the gudgeon pin and the piston crown. Two of these are compression rings which prevent blow-by of combustion gases past the piston.

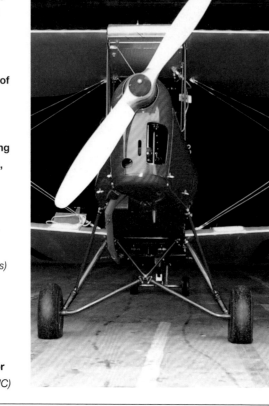

The third, the one nearest the gudgeon pin, is a scraper ring and has a small recess to allow oil to drain via ring groove drillings into the piston and little-end bearings.

All four cylinders are cooled by air, which is directed around the barrels via an arrangement of baffles from the air intake on the port side of the nose. The air first enters down the port side of the engine before reaching a backplate which closes the rear of the scoop, causing a build-up of pressure. It is then forced through the baffles between the cylinders to the low-pressure area on the starboard side, ensuring even cooling of the cylinders, before the warm air is exhausted from the rear of the cowling.

Cylinder heads and valve gear

Like the cylinder barrels, the cylinder heads are also externally finned for cooling, and each of the four castings additionally supports the pedestals for the rocker gear which actuates the inlet and exhaust valves. The earliest type of Mk1 aluminium bronze cylinder heads are easily recognised by their bronze colour and the absence of cooling fins around the inlet port.

These heads, unless modified by the fitment of stainless steel valve seats, suffer serious erosion from the leaded aviation fuels in general use today. The later aluminium-alloy cylinder heads, which feature screwed-in or shrunk-in steel valve seats, are more resilient to such fuels.

The inlet and exhaust ports are on the starboard side of each cylinder head, with the valves being actuated by rockers driven by pushrods running down the port side of the engine from the camshaft. Each inlet and exhaust

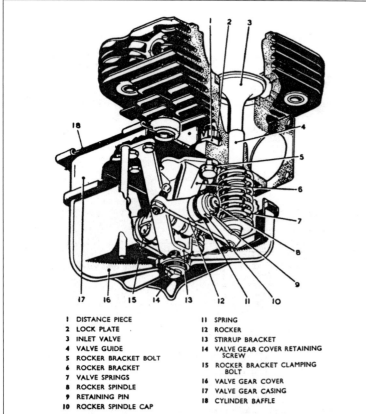

1	DISTANCE PIECE	11	SPRING
2	LOCK PLATE	12	ROCKER
3	INLET VALVE	13	STIRRUP BRACKET
4	VALVE GUIDE	14	VALVE GEAR COVER RETAINING SCREW
5	ROCKER BRACKET BOLT	15	ROCKER BRACKET CLAMPING BOLT
6	ROCKER BRACKET	16	VALVE GEAR COVER
7	VALVE SPRINGS	17	VALVE GEAR CASING
8	ROCKER SPINDLE	18	CYLINDER BAFFLE
9	RETAINING PIN		
10	ROCKER SPINDLE CAP		

valve is closed by two concentric valve springs.

There is no lubrication feed to the valve rockers and tappets. Each of the four rocker covers forms a bath which is part-filled with engine oil at the time of each tappet adjustment. This oil is then replenished at the next tappet checks, originally specified at 25 flying-hour intervals but more normally undertaken nowadays at 50 hours.

three-jet system with a butterfly throttle valve which, combined with an overlap between the operation of the slow-running and main jet systems, prevents flat spots when opening the throttle from low power settings. A power jet supplements the main jet during full throttle operation, richening the engine mixture to prevent overheating or pre-ignition.

Originally most Tiger Moths were fitted with a supplementary manual mixture control, known as the 'altitude control', next to the throttle lever, to

Fuel system

Throughout its life the Gipsy Major utilised the Claudel Hobson AI48 downdraft carburettor, attached to an inlet manifold on the starboard side of the engine and fed with fuel by gravity from the 19-gallon (86-litre) fuel tank in the upper wing centre section.

Based on a license from Claudel, a French designer, this carburettor was developed by the Wolverhampton company H.M. Hobson. The first Claudel-type carburettor had been fitted by Hobson on a Wright Flyer aeroplane in 1910.

The Hobson AI48 carburettor utilises a

ABOVE: This Claudel Hobson AI 48 carburettor, built in the 1940s, is still brand new and has yet to be fitted to an engine! (Geoff Collins)

RIGHT: The three main jets can be seen behind the air pressure balance pipe in the air inlet tract. (Geoff Collins)

RIGHT: In addition to opening the throttle, cranks attached to the throttle linkage automatically retard the ignition when the throttle is closed, to prevent the propeller kicking back during starting. (Geoff Collins)

RIGHT: To richen the mixture and allow the engine to be started from cold, a brass plunger is pressed to depress the carburettor float and 'flood' the float chamber. (Geoff Collins)

admit additional air to lean the mixture for more economical cruising or to prevent the engine running over-rich in thinner air at higher altitudes. Today, as most Tiger Moths operate at lower levels, this mixture control is usually to be found disconnected and locked in the fully rich position.

The opening of the throttle by the pilot is actuated by a series of push-pull rods and cross-shafts linking the carburettor to throttle levers on the port side of the cockpits. In addition two other controls are linked to the throttle to optimise engine performance.

A quadrant-type link between each end of the throttle control cross-shaft and the magnetos adjusts the ignition timing so that at slow running and starting the magnetos are fully retarded, minimising the risk of the propeller kicking backwards. At around one-third throttle the timing moves to fully advanced and remains in that position to allow optimum power to be delivered at the higher throttle settings.

The carburettor is fed with air via a two-position (warm air or cold air) intake which functions automatically according to throttle position. At part-throttle settings and in humid conditions there is a risk that the reduced temperature in the low-pressure area of the carburettor will cause moisture to freeze out, creating carburettor ice. This ice can 'choke' the engine, giving an over-rich mixture and causing engine failure. To reduce this risk warm air is drawn via a flame-trap element which faces the warm surface of the adjacent crankcase.

On full throttle, however, the greater density of cooler air allows more power to be produced. To take advantage of this, a flap valve inside the air intake automatically opens to allow cool air to be drawn from a small scoop on the outside of the engine cowling.

Richening the mixture for cold starting is carried out by flooding the float chamber, which is done by pressing a spring-loaded button on the top of the carburettor to depress the float. As the float chamber is flooded, fuel can usually be heard running into the pressed steel inlet manifold, followed a moment later by surplus fuel dribbling from the manifold drain elbow. Once this flow has stopped, turning over the engine four blades, with the ignition switched off and the throttle fully closed, will normally provide a sufficiently rich mixture to start a cold engine.

Ignition system

Ignition is provided by two BTH magnetos driven by gears from the rear of the engine. Both port and starboard magnetos operate independently, each feeding the four spark plugs on its side of the engine. Thus if one magneto or part of the ignition circuit were to fail, the engine's four cylinders would continue

RIGHT: The Gipsey Major ignition system. *(deHMC)*

BELOW:

1 Magnetos are permanently 'live', and as a further fail-safe against an in-flight wiring failure rely on being earthed to 'turn off'.

2 This (right-hand) magneto features a small spring clip, just above the contact breaker points, which shorts the magneto if the cap is removed.

3 This earlier (left-hand) magneto doesn't have the clip, and the aircraft ignition would be 'live' if the protective cap were to be removed. Note too the damage to the teeth on the magneto drive gear, perhaps caused by persistent backfiring.

4 Vintech have devised this test rig to spin rebuilt magnetos and monitor their spark performance. This time exposure shows that all four spark plugs are being fed with voltage.

5 This is the traditional method of securing the ignition lead to the spark plug. However, the need to minimise radio interference now means that many aircraft are fitted with shielded leads and suppressor caps. *(All Geoff Collins)*

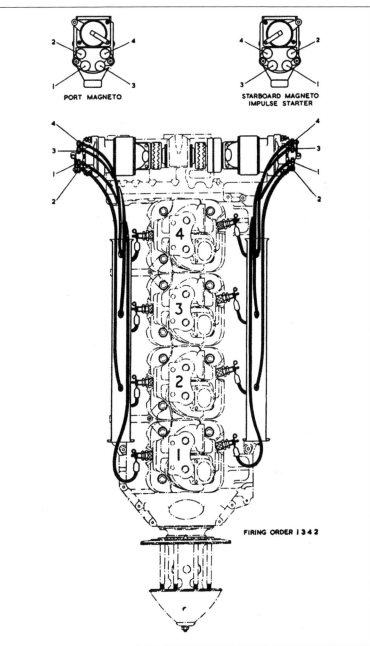

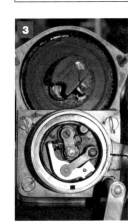

to run on sparks from the other magneto.

To aid starting, the starboard magneto only is fitted with a spring-loaded impulse device. This 'holds back' the magneto, retarding the ignition as the engine reaches its firing point at top dead centre, then trips to give a momentary forward rotation, ensuring that a powerful spark is supplied to the starboard side plugs, regardless of the speed of the engine.

Operation of the 'impulse' is normally accompanied by a distinct *click*. If this sound is missing during the starting process, it means that the impulse pawl is sticking. Starting will be impossible until it is released by giving the impulse unit body a light tap.

BELOW: Steel tube front and rear fuselage sections... *(De Havilland Maintenance and Repair Manual)*

Over the years the legend has built up that in *extremis* this can be administered even with the heel of one's shoe. However, doing so risks hitting not the alloy impulse casing but the more fragile Bakelite insulating cover. Many Tiger

Moth owners therefore use a small lightweight hammer or the handle of a screwdriver, to avoid the possibility of causing unnecessary damage.

An ignition harness on each side of the engine carries the impulses to the sparking plugs. Originally these leads were unshielded and simply secured to the spark plugs with a brass ferrule and clip. However, in order to prevent radio interference many aircraft today utilise shielded plug leads and suppressed ignition caps.

Fuselage

The main fuselage frame is constructed in three sections, using various gauges of mainly $7/8$in (22.2mm) round and $7/8$in square section T45 low-carbon steel tube, which is welded to form individual rigid structures which are bolted together. The engine mounts, forward fuselage and rear fuselage can therefore be replaced individually to speed repairs.

The core of the airframe is the forward fuselage, to which the engine, centre section struts, lower wing mountings, undercarriage and rear fuselage are bolted. It also makes up the cockpit area, to which the wooden floor, seats and 'control box' containing the linkages for all the primary aircraft controls are bolted.

The two main parts of the forward fuselage are the side frames, which when assembled to cross-members form the parallel sides of a box structure 7ft 2in (2.18m) long.

The front of each side frame is raked backward to reflect the slope of the non-structural aluminium engine firewall, while the top longerons provide the mounting points for the steel centre-section struts supporting the upper wings.

The two side frames are separated by steel tube cross-members and two 8mm diameter steel tie-rods. These tubes brace the floor, being bolted via flanged end fittings to the lower longerons at the point where the downward tubes coincide, to provide attachment areas for the root ends of the lower wings.

The forward points of the lower side frames also take vertical loads from the undercarriage and act as a mounting for the oil tank. The front of each side frame also bolts to two triangulated square-section tubular frames which form the

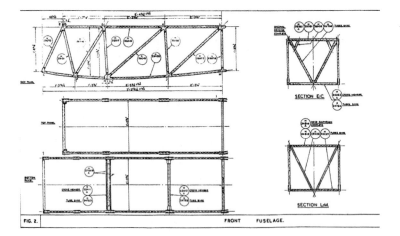

FIG. 2. FRONT FUSELAGE.

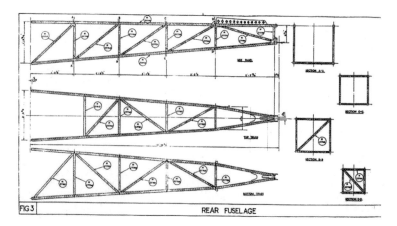

FIG 3 REAR FUSELAGE

LEFT AND ABOVE: …seen here looking from the front backwards, bolt together to create the main fuselage structure. *(Andy Smith)*

BELOW: The final assembly of these Tiger Moths at Bankstown, New South Wales, shows the evolution from basic frame to complete aeroplane. *(deHMC)*

RIGHT: Along with the
fuselage side frames
and cross-members,
two steel tie rods…
(Geoff Collins)

BELOW: …take the
vertical and lateral loads
from the cantilevered
engine mountings, the
lower wing roots, the
cabane struts and the
undercarriage.
(Andy Smith)

RIGHT: The control
box ready to return to
the aeroplane in 'as
new' condition after
renovation by Matthew
Boddington in his
Sywell workshops.
(Stephen Slater)

engine mounts at the front of the airframe. The engine mounts extend 3ft (0.91m) ahead of the bulkhead on each side of the aeroplane and contain four receptacles for rubber engine mountings, two on each side, which correspond to the cast alloy 'feet' attached to the crankcase of the Gipsy Major engine.

The complete forward fuselage cage is completed at the front and rear by upper and lower cross-members and diagonal bracing to provide a surprisingly light and rigid unit. To this, a total of 40 2BA bolts and nuts secure the plywood floor, to which in turn is fixed the control box that forms a central spine at the base of the cockpits, upon which the seats are bolted and on each side of which the occupants place their feet.

The spruce and plywood control box acts as a single mounting point for all the primary flight controls and is removable as a unit for repairs or maintenance. The front and rear control columns are linked by a torque tube and a connecting rod which run the length of the control box, through both cockpits.

For the elevator control, a cross-shaft with integral levers immediately behind the rear seat is operated by a short pushrod from the rear control column and is connected directly to the control cables running to the tail of the aircraft. A downward-projecting lever on the torque tube between the two columns operates the aileron cables externally, under the cockpit floor. The rudder controls too are mounted on the control box and are coupled by connecting rods. The ends of the rear rudder bar extend out of each side of the cockpit and the external control cables run direct to 'horns' on each side of the rudder.

The rear fuselage section is likewise made up of four ⁷/₈in (22.2mm) square T45 steel tube longerons, which taper through five reinforced bays to a single sternpost at the rear. Built on a jig as a single, rigid, 11ft (3.35m) welded-up unit, it is designed to be simply bolted in place on the rear of the side frames and carries the drillings for the wooden top decking and the mountings for the tail surfaces.

The top decking, made of curved moulded wood over ply formers, forms the upper surface of the fuselage, cockpit areas and rear fuselage. Bolted into place on the fuselage frames, it completes a robust fuselage structure that is both easy to assemble and easy to repair. These are attributes which allow even quite badly damaged Tiger Moths to be repaired according to the manufacturer's approved repair schemes.

The majority of accident damage to Tiger Moth fuselages is usually, as in the past, to one or both of the lower side frames in the vicinity of the undercarriage compression leg attachment. These most commonly suffer distortion from excessively heavy landings.

If an even heavier accident has occurred, they may also suffer lateral distortion from the loads applied if a wingtip has struck the ground. As with any structural repair, in addition to repairing the immediate damage one should always carefully check the adjacent structure and welds for cracking, in case the loads have been transferred.

A severe nose-over or heavy landing may have also resulted in bending of the engine mounts and even the front end of the fuselage frame. Once again, the modular nature of the frames means that repair is generally practicable. A similar heavy landing in a wooden-framed DH60 Moth can result in the entire forward fuselage breaking away.

At the rear of the airframe, corrosion is a potential enemy. While few if any Tiger Moths are today condemned to living outdoors, they were in the past, and any moisture taken on board will inevitably head to the lowest part of the airframe.

In a Tiger Moth, as in any 'taildragger', the lowest part of the airframe is the tail, and the complex union of longerons, reinforcing tubes and sternpost is the most likely host to corrosion. This is further encouraged by the fact that the fabric is directly attached to the frame at this point, potentially holding any moisture against the steel tubes. A close and regular scheme of inspection is obviously a wise precaution.

In wartime military service some repairs such as temporarily 'sleeving' damaged longerons were deemed acceptable. However, this is not the case today.

All welding of the fuselage, whether to replace corroded tubes or repair accident damage, must be carried out by a certified airframe welder. The

LEFT: **The curved plywood top decking of the DH82A took advantage of wood-forming techniques that would later be used to construct the de Havilland Mosquito.** (Andy Smith)

ABOVE: **This rear fuselage, awaiting restoration at Sywell shows the classic signs of light corrosion and earlier accident repair.** (Andy Smith)

good news is that a number of these experts have the necessary jigs to ensure perfect alignment of the finished components.

Undercarriage

Quaintly still described in many manuals as 'the alighting gear', the Tiger Moth undercarriage is another example of elegant engineering simplicity. The main structure is made up of two tubular steel split-axles, which are pivoted from a tripod steel tube structure under the centre of the fuselage.

The majority of the landing loads are, however, taken by two compression legs which extend from the axles close to the wheels to fittings on the lower fuselage longerons which double as the bottom wing front spar attachments. These compression legs each contain a spring and a bronze friction damper beneath a streamlined fairing.

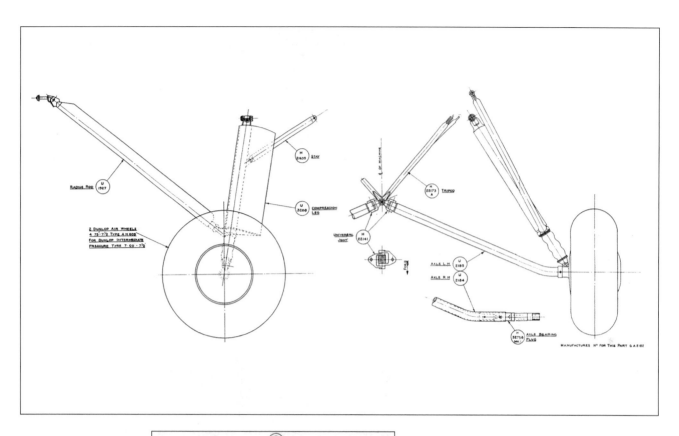

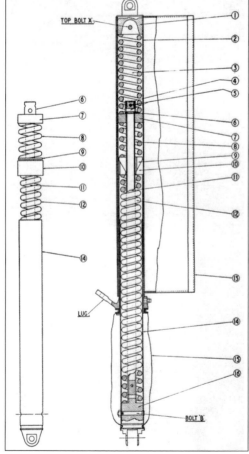

Fore and aft loads are accommodated by radius rods, which extend from the forward fuselage to the bottom of the compression legs, while some additional damping of the undercarriage is provided by the 7½in x 7in low-pressure tyres. Fitted on Dunlop alloy wheels, these are inflated to 12–15psi (0.84–1.05 bar).

The result is a simple yet – as countless student pilots will testify – robust and relatively forgiving undercarriage. It is, in the case of most Tiger Moths, without brakes. The aeroplane relies instead on the braking effect of a cast-iron shoe at the base of the sprung tailskid, which is steered via fittings at the bottom of the rudder.

The tailskid undercarriage was designed with grass airfields in mind and works remarkably well on such surfaces. However, with the advent of tarmac runways and large concrete aprons Canadian-built Tiger Moths led the way in the fitment of a sprung, fully-castoring 4in (100mm) diameter tail-wheel assembly.

Bendix drum brakes were fitted to the main-wheels, with control cables leading up the compression struts to a differential brake control via a hand-lever mounted in each

ABOVE: The tubular split-axle undercarriage incorporates coil springs and a friction damper, with added suspension provided by 7½in x 7in low-pressure tyres. (Geoff Collins)

BELOW: The undercarriage is the fastest-wearing item on Tiger Moths in regular service. (Geoff Collins)

LEFT: The lower fuselage longerons double as the bottom wing front spar attachments, as well as absorbing the loads from the undercarriage. (Geoff Collins)

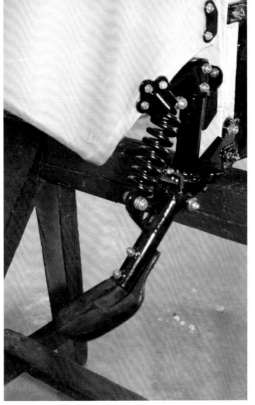

LEFT: With the exception of Tiger Moths built in Canada, wheel brakes were not normally fitted. The aeroplane relies instead on the braking effect of a replaceable cast-iron shoe on the sprung and steerable tailskid. (Andy Smith)

BELOW: This Tiger Moth converted to use the 'Canadian' tail-wheel undercarriage shows off the distinctive forward canting of the undercarriage legs designed to reduce the risk of nosing over if the brakes are applied heavily. (Brian A. Marshall)

RIGHT: Each of the
four mainplanes is
built around two
I-section spruce spars.
(deHMC)

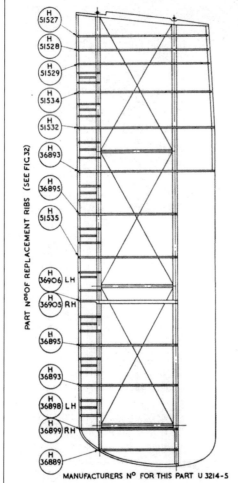

RIGHT: The wing is
braced internally by
compression struts
between the spars
and diagonal bracing
wires. The final shape
is given by 11 ribs in
each upper and 13 ribs
in each lower wing. (De
Havilland Maintenance
and Repair Manual)

PART Nºs OF REPLACEMENT RIBS (SEE FIG 32)

H 51527
H 51528
H 51529
H 51534
H 51532
H 36893
H 36895
H 51535
H 36906 LH
H 36905 RH
H 36895
H 36893
H 36898 LH
H 36899 RH
H 36889

MANUFACTURERS Nº FOR THIS PART U 3214-5

cockpit. In order to minimise the risk of 'nosing over' due to harsh application of the brakes, Canadian-built Tiger Moths had their main-wheels moved slightly further forwards by the simple expedient of slight shortening the undercarriage radius rods.

Traditional woodwork

The wings, the tail unit and the top decking of the fuselage are traditionally built structures manufactured from fabric-covered spruce spars, leading edges and trailing edges, along with spruce and plywood formers and ribs. These are then given their structural strength by internal and external bracing. This is literally the same type of structure as was successfully utilised in the pioneering days of flight by the Wright brothers.

Each of the four mainplanes is built around two one-piece I-section spruce wing spars, which provide the main structural strength of the wing. They are braced internally by three compression struts interposed between front and rear spars and diagonal wire bracing within the wing structure. The wing spars are additionally strengthened by ash 'doublers' in the vicinity of the points, where steel fittings

transmit the loads from the interplane struts, landing wires and flying wires.

As with any wooden components used in aircraft construction, all timber must be of certified aircraft quality, free of all knots, and must meet specific requirements in terms of moisture content, grain count, grain inclination, brittleness and strength. All approved timber is issued with a release note by its supplier, which is then kept in the airframe records for future inspection.

Fortunately supplies of aircraft-quality timber remain readily available. Even the substantial spruce wing spars are available in pre-cut and drilled form from specialist suppliers in Canada and New Zealand.

The wing's aerodynamic shape is created by fabricated wooden wing ribs, with 11 ribs in each upper and 13 in each lower wing. Each wing rib is made up of approximately 30 small pieces of lightweight spruce and ply, glued and secured with brass pins to form the aerofoil section of the wing.

Each rib is slid into position along the wing spars before the whole wing structure is carefully trammelled square by tensioning the diagonal bracing wires inside each wing. Each wire includes an Avro-type strap turnbuckle, the wire itself including two wire ferrules and the

RIGHT: When the wire bracing is fully tensioned and the wing correctly aligned, each rib is secured in place on the spars by the use of metal clips. *(Stephen Slater)*

RIGHT: The wingtip is given its shape by an aluminium tube bent in a jig to give the correct radii. *(Stephen Slater)*

RIGHT: Small 'riblets' give the leading edge of the wing additional strength. *(Stephen Slater)*

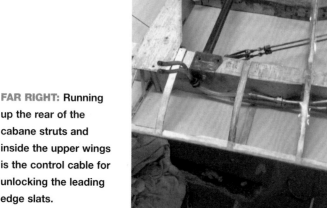

FAR RIGHT: Running up the rear of the cabane struts and inside the upper wings is the control cable for unlocking the leading edge slats. *(Geoff Collins)*

shackle and two clevis pins. Certain wires in the inner wing bays can alternatively be made in the form of a rod threaded left-hand and right-hand at opposite ends.

Only when the wing has been trammelled square are the ribs wood-screwed in position, using steel rib clips which fit over each rib at its intersection with the two wing spars. The shape of the leading edge of each wing is also formed by a series of riblets which fit between the main ribs and extend from the spruce leading edge to the front spar. In the case of Tiger Moths built in Australia and Canada, added strength is given to the leading edges by the use of a plywood skin under the fabric.

The outer tip of each wing is given its shape by an aluminium tube, formed in a jig to create a wingtip bow, while the inner ends of the lower wing carry additional supporting ribs and an external plywood walkway for access to the cockpits. Both lower wings contain internal mountings for the spruce and plywood 'aileron box' which contains the differential aileron controls.

The aileron control cables are carried in the lower wings from the fuselage to the aileron control box. They are then attached to the ends of a short drive chain, which engages on the geared crank, which controls the aileron itself by a pushrod.

The rear spars of the lower wings act as the mountings for the aileron hinges.

The ailerons themselves are constructed from a spruce spar and trailing edge, linked by six identical intermediate ribs, a heavier inner rib, and a shorter tip rib, the end of which is attached to a formed aluminium trailing edge tube.

While the construction of the upper and lower wings is similar, the upper wings are without ailerons and only contain the control cables for locking and unlocking the aluminium leading edge slots.

The upper wings are pinned and bolted to a

centre section with tubular steel carry-through members and wooden ribs either side of the space for the fuel tank. The centre section is supported above the fuselage by two N-shaped, streamline-section steel tube cabane struts, each comprising one V-shaped and one single strut each side. These are additionally cross-braced by streamlined centre-section wires. The complete centre section structure also supports the airfoil-section, 19-gallon (86-litre), soldered-steel fuel tank, which has a 'saddle' shape that enables it to sit around the front centre-section spar.

The wingspan of the Tiger Moth is 29ft 4in (8.94m). A permanent reminder of the 'trial and error' method by which the distinctive sweepback of the Tiger Moth's wings evolved is that the line of the wing ribs does not align with the airflow.

The tailplane, fin and rudder are of similar construction to the wings. The tailplane has a one-piece routed rear spar and a laminated front spar which is curved to form its leading edge. Likewise the fin has two straight spruce spars with connecting ribs, with the rear spar being extended to the base of the fuselage to form a sternpost.

Solid spruce spars are used for the leading edges of the separate elevators and for the rudder, with their distinctive shapes being formed by spruce ribs and tubular aluminium trailing edges. The tailplanes are braced for vertical loads by diagonal struts running from their undersides to the lower longerons of the rear fuselage.

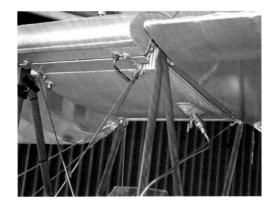

LEFT: The cabane struts and upper wing structure support the airfoil-section, 19-gallon (86.4-litre), ribbed steel fuel tank. *(Andy Smith)*

LEFT: A close look at the line of the wing ribs reveals that they are not in line with the airflow – a lasting reminder of the 'trial and error' approach to the Tiger Moth's wing sweepback. *(deHMC archive)*

BELOW: The rear fin spar is extended to form a sternpost, bolted to the rear of the fuselage, which carries the rudder hinges and sprung tailskid mechanism. *(Geoff Collins)*

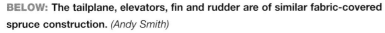

BELOW: The tailplane, elevators, fin and rudder are of similar fabric-covered spruce construction. *(Andy Smith)*

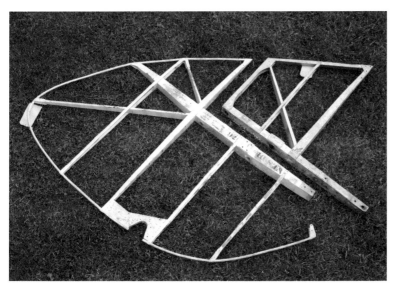

Fabric covering

While the steel tube, spruce and ply structure gives the Tiger Moths its skeleton, the final covering is what gives the aircraft its distinctive appearance and flying capability. With the exception of the propeller, engine cowling, steel struts, fuel tank and oil tank, almost every part of the Tiger Moth is covered in doped fabric.

The most traditional covering materials are cotton or 'Irish' linen, the latter being made from fibres of the flax plant, most commonly grown in Ireland, Italy and Belgium. When combined with doping agents such as cellulose acetate or cellulose acetate butyrate, either material shrinks to form a taut, light yet robust covering. It is also easy to repair, with schemes of 'field repairs' and doped-on patches allowing an

aeroplane to return to service within hours rather than days – a vital attribute in a basic trainer.

While linen or cotton coverings continue to be preferred by those who seek originality, their high cost combined with the finite life of all cover materials – which have to be stripped off and replaced on a regular basis – have made synthetic fabric coverings such as Poly-Fiber and Ceconite an increasingly attractive alternative.

Of course, it is vital before re-covering or repairing an aircraft to confirm that a fabric of equal quality and strength to the original is used, and that any change of fabric type is approved by the airworthiness authority concerned.

Traditionally aircraft fabric is glued, sewn or laced to the airframe structure, and then doped to tauten, seal and protect it. In original service, pre-manufactured 'bags' were produced, creating a single unit of fabric which would be slipped over the rear fuselage, wings or tail surfaces to speed the covering process. Today it is more likely that rolls of fabric will be used to cover a single surface at a time. Whether traditional linen covering and dope is used, or a modern synthetic covering shrunk to fit by means of a heat gun or an iron, the basic principles and skills remain the same.

The first step is to reduce the risk of fretting or premature wear of the covering by ensuring that every part of the aircraft which comes into contact with the fabric is free from upstanding or sharp-edged features. This may require an additional strip of fabric to be glued, doped or sewn on, or a self-adhesive tape to be applied for anti-chafe purposes. Once this check is completed, the main layer of fabric covering is cut to shape, slightly oversize, using pinking shears to provide a serrated edge and thereby reduce fraying.

If a single piece of fabric is insufficiently large, pieces can be joined together by sewing, with the seam ideally running in line with the airflow. A double-folded 'balloon seam' (itself dating to the dawn of human flight) is used to join the fabric sections. Traditionally, fabric is carried continuously around the leading edge and then the top and bottom surfaces are joined together by hand-stitching along the trailing edge.

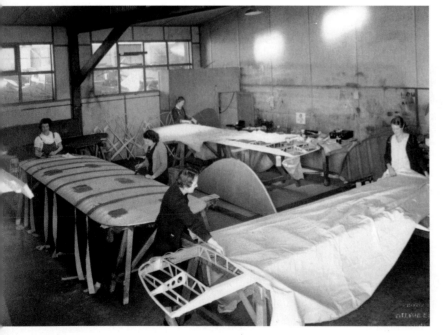

The following sequence of images from the Newnes airframe training manual of 1938 show the process of laying additional supporting strips over prominent areas such as wing ribs and doping them in position.

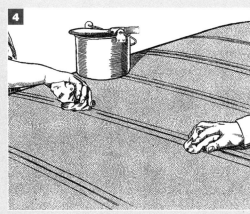

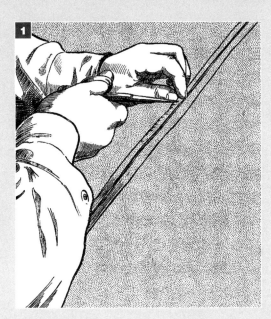

1 Linen strips being serrated to permit seams to lay flat.

2 After 'stringing' has been completed, the work is given a coating of red dope, which tautens the fabric. Seams and lines of 'stringing' then receive an additional coat of dope.

3 The strips of fabric are now laid on the still-tacky dope and rubbed down.

4 The strip is rubbed down until the dope begins to ooze through, when it is given a final coat of red dope, producing a strong watertight seal.

5 Showing the doping strips. Note the serrated edges to give greater adhesion and to prevent peeling off.

6 Where small bores or windows are required, these are made by using 'doping patches'.

7 The final operation, spraying the fabric with a non-tautening paint of the desired colour.

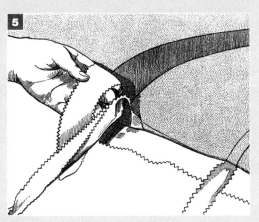

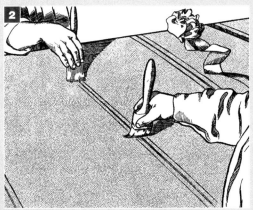

RIGHT: 'Balloon stitching', with a double fold in the fabric, was in use even before the introduction of powered flight. It is still the preferred method of joining two pieces of fabric.

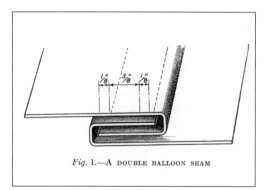

Fig. 1.—A DOUBLE BALLOON SEAM

ABOVE RIGHT: These inspection panels are placed in the fabric to facilitate later inspection of the wing structure and otherwise hidden cables. *(Geoff Collins)*

The covering is then water-shrunk and when dry given its first coat of dope, which will further tauten the surface as it dries. In areas subject to aerodynamic loads such as the wings and the tail unit, the fabric is stitched to the ribs using special braided waxed cotton thread and Egyptian Tape reinforcing. This is sewn through the fabric and around the wing rib at a pitch

of 3in (75mm) and then covered by additional strips of serrated fabric tape doped in place. Subsequent layers of dope and paint will then provide the final finish, although it should always be remembered that dope and paint add weight, and that too much can affect the aeroplane's performance.

Rigging, flying and landing wires

Perhaps the most daunting process to be faced by anyone rebuilding a biplane will be the final assembly and 'rigging' to ensure that it is both dimensionally correct and that the loads carried by the wing spars, fuselage mountings, struts and bracing wires are equally distributed.

The first step is to level the aeroplane by placing it on trestles with the undercarriage clear of the ground. If the engine is fitted, it is good practice at this stage to add a weight to the tailskid to prevent the aeroplane from nosing over, as with the tail raised it is close to the point of balance. Sadly, many a pristine rudder has been dented as the tail has ascended gracefully into the hangar roof!

Ensuring that the fuselage is horizontal is aided by two datum bolts on the starboard-side fuselage top longeron. Lateral levels are checked by using a straight-edge and level placed under and across the top longerons.

Next the centre-section struts are bolted into place either side, and the centre section is fitted and braced by securing the streamlined bracing wires to the wiring plates beneath the centre-

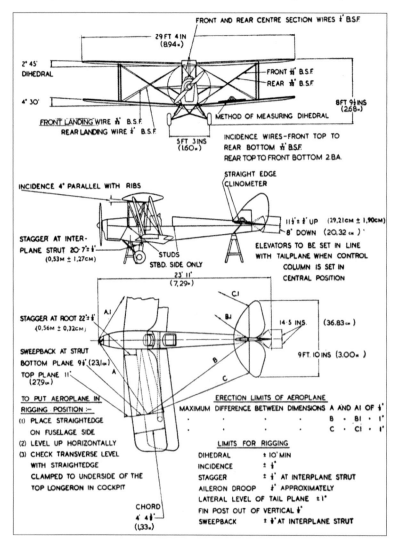

LEFT: Rigging diagram from 1944 Maintenance and Repair Manual. *(deHMC)*

LEFT: Before the rigging process begins the aeroplane is positioned with the fuselage horizontal and the wings level, with the aid of a spirit level and a straight edge. Plumb lines are then dropped from the leading edge of the wing. The centre section is rigged first, then the alignments are adjusted outwards along the wing to prevent undue loads being placed on the centre section. *(Ian Castle)*

section cross-members. The centre section is then aligned by rotating the bracing wires in their left- and right-hand-threaded fork ends to adjust their length.

The correct orientation of the centre section with the fuselage is checked by dropping four plumb lines from the eyebolts at the ends of the centre-section spars. These are adjusted until the distances are equal to the sides of the fuselage.

The stagger – the forward relationship of the upper wing to the lower – is checked by measuring the distances from the forward plumb lines to the centre line of the bottom front spar fitting on the lower fuselage. This should be 1ft 10in +/– $\frac{1}{8}$in (558mm +/– 3mm), with both distances equal for each side.

Only when the cabane structure is correctly rigged should the rigging of the mainplanes proceed, and the cabane rigging should be regularly rechecked. Any attempt to adjust wing rigging with the cabanes out of tolerance can place excessive loads on flying wires and wing spars, leading to potential structural failure.

The assembly and rigging of the mainplanes begins by lifting one top wing into position, with the wingtip being supported by trestles or by hand as the roots' ends are attached to the centre section. Next the lower wing is fitted and the two interplane struts are secured to their sockets on the upper and lower spars.

The wings remain supported by a trestle as the landing wires, flying wires and incidence wires are loosely fitted, and then the assembly process is repeated for the opposite pair of wings. Some restorers actually 'box' the wings, assembling the complete structure of mainplanes, struts and wires before introducing them as a single unit to the fuselage.

With the wings and struts in position, now comes the challenge of achieving the required rigging of incidence, dihedral and stagger by gently adjusting the length and tension of the external bracing wires. These are all specially-made, rolled, aerodynamic-section wires with threaded ends that allow adjustment relative to the forked end fittings which secure them to the fuselage, wings and struts.

Two landing wires on each side of the aeroplane extend from the top of the rear centre-section struts to the lower interplane

LEFT: The specially-made, streamline-section flying and landing wires are fitted with threaded ends that allow adjustment of their length relative to their fittings on the fuselage, wings and struts. *(Geoff Collins)*

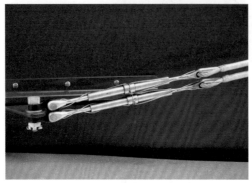

RIGHT: Where any rigging wires cross they are protected from chafing by small fibre pads, stitched into position. *(Geoff Collins)*

RIGHT: All rigging and control cable joints are securely wire-locked to prevent them loosening due to vibration. *(Geoff Collins)*

struts. These form a triangular structure to carry the downward load of the wings when they are not generating lift. Flying wires meanwhile extend from the bottom wing front spar root-end attachment to the fuselage to the top end of each interplane strut, accommodating the

upward load from the wings when in the air.

The incidence wires, which cross diagonally between the front and rear interplane struts, provide bracing in torsion to maintain the same incidence of the top and bottom wings at the struts as at the root end. All the wires are protected from chafing by small fibre pads at the points where they cross, and the landing and flying wires on each side of the aeroplane are additionally supported by wooden 'acorns' which act as a spreader bar at the intersection of the wires.

Only one company in the world today continues to produce streamline wires for use in Tiger Moths. Bruntons of Musselburgh, a few miles from the city of Edinburgh, has a century-long history of producing bracing and control cables for aviation.

In addition to providing stainless steel streamline section wires for Tiger Moths in response to batch orders co-ordinated by the de Havilland Moth Club, Bruntons have also recently discovered a new market for their streamline section wires. They have increasingly been used to provide streamline rigging for racing yachts and by Formula One motor racing teams as the most aerodynamically efficient means of bracing bodywork and airfoils.

Propeller

One of the Tiger Moth's most distinctive features is its handsome laminated two-blade wooden propeller. While some – particularly those on Tiger Moths restored to represent aircraft in military service – have their craftsmanship hidden beneath an authentic black-painted surface, many owners today opt instead for a varnished finish, to show off the sheer beauty and precision of woodworking which is now a little-known art.

Originally three types of wooden propeller were developed for the Tiger Moth. They were designed by de Havilland, but made by outside suppliers, including the Airscrew Company of Weybridge in Surrey, Lang Propellers of Peterborough and Hordern Richmond Aircraft in Buckinghamshire, as well as locally in Australia, New Zealand and Canada.

All three approved designs were of 76in

RIGHT: The markings on the boss of this propeller on the first DH82A, G-ACDA, identify it as having been made by Lang Propeller of Chesham in Buckinghamshire in September 1939. It is of the standard 6ft 4in or 76in (1.93m) diameter, but has a 4ft 11in pitch, slightly coarser than the norm for RAF trainers, allowing more relaxed cruising. *(Geoff Collins)*

ABOVE: The core of the propeller is built up to seven hardwood laminates, glued and clamped, before being milled to create the final profile. *(Stephen Slater)*

These pictures taken at de Havilland's propeller works at Rongotai in New Zealand in 1940 show the complete manufacturing process: the creation of the initial laminates, their compression and gluing, shaping and, finally, balancing. *(deHMC archive)*

(1.93m) diameter, but had different pitches depending on use. The standard DH propeller had a 55in (1.4m) pitch, meaning, in the hypothetical case of 100 per cent efficiency, that 55in would be covered in forward flight for every revolution of the blade.

Coarser 57in (1.5m) and 59in (1.45m) propellers were also produced. These allowed reduced engine revs in cruising flight, but came at the expense of poorer take-off and climb performance.

Today Tiger Moth aircraft are approved to fly with propellers having pitches between 42 and 65in (1.08 and 1.65m). Ultra-fine pitches below 53in (1.35m) have been used on aircraft with special slow-speed applications such as banner-towing or glider tugs. These can be equated to the use of a low gear in an automobile, allowing higher revs at the expense of forward speed.

Most propellers were originally manufactured from a combination of walnut and mahogany, relatively densely-grained woods which have the least likelihood of change due to moisture content. As with all wooden propellers, up to seven laminates are glued and clamped together to cure, before being milled to create the correct shape.

While this process was first achieved using hand tools in conjunction with cross-sectional templates to determine the exact shape and profile, as Tiger Moth production increased a variety of machines were created to accurately obtain the final shape. Some of these could even produce multiple propellers in one process.

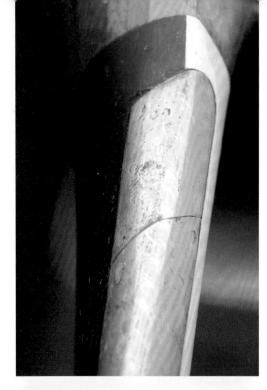

RIGHT: A brass reinforcing strip protects the leading edge of the propeller from abrasion. *(Geoff Collins)*

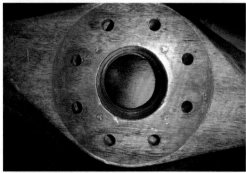

RIGHT: The eight concentric bolt holes allow fitment to the propeller flange… *(Stephen Slater)*

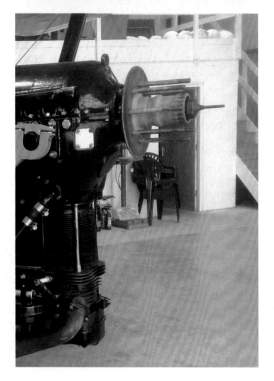

RIGHT: …which is in turn keyed and bolted to the nose of the crankshaft. *(Stephen Slater)*

After completion of the final shaping and inspection of the product, the final drill holes were created in the hub, brass reinforcing strips were added to the leading edge, and the tips and multiple coats of paint or varnish were applied. The final part of the production process placed the propeller on a knife-edge balancing device, with a small lead plug close to the boss being used to achieve precise balance.

During the war years, supplies of hardwoods such as walnut and mahogany became scarce. Hordern Richmond Aircraft of Chesham in Buckinghamshire therefore gained approval for a patent method which used locally-cut birchwood laminates coated with a hard resin, on to which a celluloid 'stocking' was bonded under pressure in a large autoclave. This process produced significant quantities of Tiger Moth propellers and was also used for wooden propeller blades fitted to aircraft such as the Spitfire and Mosquito.

An indication of the quality of the wartime production methods is that some original propellers are still in use on Tiger Moths today. However, age, damage and general wear have led to modern replacements increasingly being required. Perhaps the most spectacular are those produced in New South Wales, Australia, by Invincible Airscrews. Produced to original de Havilland drawings, these stand out from the crowd due to their use of varnished mahogany laminates and burnished brass leading edges.

Another supplier is the Belgian maker Establissement Poncelet, whose tradition of wooden propeller production dates back to the company's foundation in 1932. Now managed by Roger Poncelet, the third generation of the family, the company also make boats and wind generators, but the propeller-making tradition continues both for vintage types and for a modern generation of microlight and sport aircraft.

Perhaps the most numerous propellers in use on Tiger Moths today are those produced from laminates of ash with an integral brass leading edge guard, a trailing edge strengthened for hand-swinging and an epoxy resin finish. Ironically, these propellers for the most British of flying machines are produced in deepest Bavaria, by the Hoffman company of Rosenheim.

LEFT: In the 1930s and 1940s every aircraft factory would have had a bustling woodworking workshop. Here spruce planks are being turned into wing spars. (deHMC archive)

Wood – nature's composite

The Tiger Moth's fabric-covered wooden wings and tail unit may have stemmed from a bygone era, yet they were perfectly suited for the aeroplane's training role, where durability and repairability were the prime requirements. These attributes of wooden construction continue to benefit owners today.

Unlike metal, wood has an infinite fatigue life and damaged structures can often be repaired more easily. Tiger Moths continue to be refurbished cost-effectively when more modern types can be beyond economical repair.

However, the type of wood and the way it is prepared is of vital importance. There is probably no other form of wooden construction anywhere in the world which places a higher emphasis on the structural strength and quality of the material than that required from aircraft timber. Inevitably no two trees will grow in exactly the same way, but the type of wood used, its selection and the quality of its preparation makes a critical difference to likely strength. All wood used in a Tiger Moth, or any other aeroplane, must be of certified aircraft quality, verified by a release note issued by an approved supplier.

The most important components of the wooden structure of a Tiger Moth – the eight

CENTRE: Even a wing in very poor condition can still form a basis for restoration. In addition to crash damage, this wing had become home to a large colony of field mice while in storage! (Stephen Slater)

BELOW: This wing is all-new, fabricated from modern supplies of aircraft-quality spruce. (Stephen Slater)

wing spars (two to each wing), along with the spars which give structural strength to the ailerons, fin, rudder, tailplane and elevators – are shaped from planks of Sitka Spruce, softwood from a tall conifer which grows predominantly in North America.

Sitka Spruce is particularly noted for having a uniform texture and a straight grain, reducing the risk of ingrown defects which could weaken its structural properties. The distinctive shape of a mature spruce tree, with a long straight trunk up to 80m (260ft) tall, but with branches only in the top half, ensures that wood from the lower trunk is largely free of imperfections and knot-holes in the grain which can be formed by branches stemming out from the trunk.

Another big advantage of spruce is its ability to combine strength with a relatively low weight. It typically has a density of around 440kg/m³, as compared with Douglas Fir – another wood used for aircraft construction – which has a typical density of over 510kg/m³. If all eight wing spars were to be made from Douglas Fir the combined weight of the wing structures could be expected to rise from around 75kg to nearly 90kg, with a proportionate effect on the aircraft's performance.

Mountain Ash, a hardwood used extensively in Europe in the early days of aviation, is even heavier, at around 800kg/m³. While it is particularly strong and compression-resistant, its higher weight means that, along with other dense woods such as mahogany and birch, it is used principally in the manufacture of wooden propellers and in plywood sheets used for

cockpit floors and fuselage decking.

In addition to the type of tree, the manner in which the tree has grown is also important to the future strength of the timber. The trunk of a tree has been described as a series of thousands of elongated, hollow, water-filled cells, glued together in bundles like drinking straws. The line of these cellulose fibres, which generally run parallel to the outer surface of the trunk, is the grain direction.

Each year, trees grow in girth by adding new layers around the outside periphery of the trunk. In softwoods such as spruce, this growth can be seen on the end surfaces of a cut log as concentric annual growth rings. A lighter colour represents the faster growth of the tree during the earlier growing season, while a darker colour indicates slower, denser growth during the less favourable part of the growing season.

In addition, examination of the trunk of a freshly felled tree will show two distinct zones in the cross-section. The darker inner zone, which makes up around 70 per cent of the surface area, is the heartwood, which provides the structural strength of the trunk and is the optimum choice for aircraft timber.

The lighter outer zone is the sapwood, which provides the tree's nutrient storage and is the route through which sap flows up the trunk. As the trunk expands the inner sapwood cells are gradually converted into denser, stronger, thicker-walled heartwood. Sapwood is not as dense as heartwood and the nutrients contained within it make it more prone to insect attack.

BELOW: Ash, a heavier wood, is more often used for laminates and ply structures such as the cockpit floor and upper decking. *(Stephen Slater)*

BELOW RIGHT: Quarter sawing is the acknowledged method of ensuring a straight grain along the line of a plank and provides maximum strength by utilising the heartwood of the tree trunk. *(Stephen Slater)*

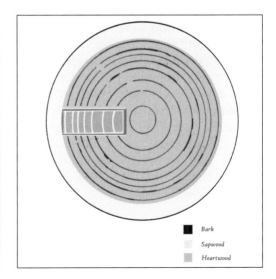

Bark

Sapwood

Heartwood

The direction in which wood is cut is also critical to the strength of a finished component. The tensile strength of timber varies with grain direction and is at its maximum parallel to the grain. Therefore a method known as 'quarter sawing' is used to ensure that the boards are cut from the trunk in such a way that the grain runs along the length of the plank and that the rings run approximately vertically through it from top to bottom. Quarter-sawn boards are more expensive to cut but are less likely to distort or crack during the curing process and will be more stable in use.

When a tree is felled the timber has a very high moisture content, and freshly-sawn lumber will lose up to 50 per cent of its total weight, shrink, and become much stronger, harder and more durable during the drying and stabilising process. The cut boards are first seasoned in hot-air drying kilns, then stored under cover in raised and separated stacks to ensure free airflow around them. Once the moisture content of the timber is stable at around 12 per cent it is regarded as cured and is ready for cutting into the finished components.

In the case of Tiger Moth wing and fin spars, the spruce used has to cope principally with compression stresses along the upper edge and tension stresses along the lower edge. In between, the spar takes sheer stresses which are much lower, consequently the solid wood in the shear area need not be so massive. The wood is therefore reduced in thickness by routing to save weight, creating a distinctive I-beam shape to the spars. The wing spars, which were originally machine-cut en masse, have accurately spindled ends to align them with the metal wing fittings.

In addition to major structural items such as the spars, spruce is extensively used

ABOVE: The production of wing ribs from many small components was labour-intensive, but in wartime it was important to use even the smallest pieces of timber which would otherwise be scrapped. *(deHMC)*

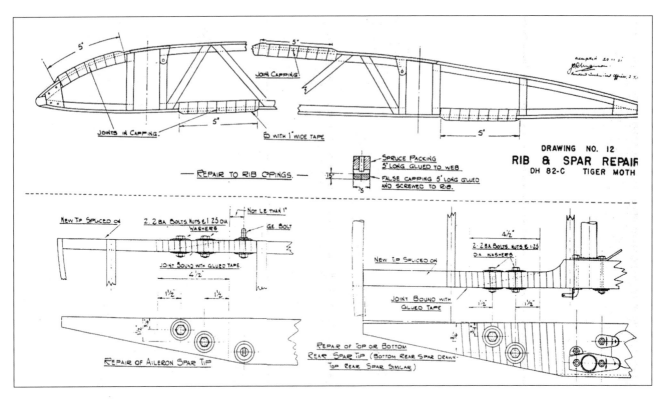

REPAIR TO RIB CPPINGS.

SPRUCE PACKING
5' LONG GLUED TO WEB

FALSE CAPPING 5' LONG GLUED
AND SCREWED TO RIB.

DRAWING NO. 12
RIB & SPAR REPAIR
DH 82-C TIGER MOTH

NEW TIP SPLICED ON

2. 2 BA BOLTS NUTS & 1 25 DIA WASHERS

GE BOLT

NOT LE THAN 1"

JOINT BOUND WITH GLUED TAPE.

REPAIR OF AILERON SPAR TIP

NEW TIP SPLICED ON

2. 2 BA BOLTS NUTS & 1.25 DIA WASHERS

JOINT BOUND WITH GLUED TAPE

REPAIR OF TOP OR BOTTOM REAR SPAR TIP (BOTTOM REAR SPAR DRAWN TOP REAR SPAR SIMILAR)

EXTENT OF DAMACE REPAIRABLE BY THIS METHOD.
SPLIT IN WEB NOT EXCEEDING 1 1/2 IN LENGTH & 1/16 IN DEPTH, OR CUM POCKET 1/4 IN WIDTH & 1/8 IN DEPTH, PROVIDED THAT THE SPLIT OR CUM POCKET IS NOT NEARER TO THE TOP OR BOTTOM EDGES OF THE PLY BISCUIT THAN 1/3 RD OF THE WIDTH OF THE BISCUIT.

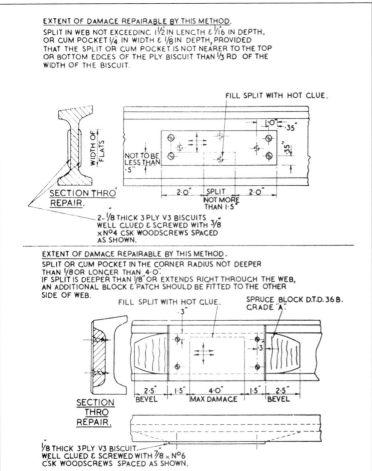

FILL SPLIT WITH HOT CLUE.

WIDTH OF FLATS

NOT TO BE LESS THAN .5"

SECTION THRO' REPAIR.

2 - 1/8 THICK 3 PLY V3 BISCUITS WELL CLUED & SCREWED WITH 3/8 × N°4 CSK WOODSCREWS SPACED AS SHOWN.

EXTENT OF DAMACE REPAIRABLE BY THIS METHOD.
SPLIT OR CUM POCKET IN THE CORNER RADIUS NOT DEEPER THAN 1/8 OR LONGER THAN 4·0.
IF SPLIT IS DEEPER THAN 1/8" OR EXTENDS RIGHT THROUGH THE WEB, AN ADDITIONAL BLOCK & PATCH SHOULD BE FITTED TO THE OTHER SIDE OF WEB.

FILL SPLIT WITH HOT CLUE.

SPRUCE BLOCK D.T.D. 36 B. CRADE 'A'

2·5" BEVEL 1·5" 4·0" MAX DAMAGE 1·5" 2·5" BEVEL

SECTION THRO REPAIR.

1/8 THICK 3 PLY V3 BISCUIT WELL CLUED & SCREWED WITH 7/8 × N°6 CSK WOODSCREWS SPACED AS SHOWN.

ABOVE: Approved repair schemes enable even major components to be repaired and replaced, as shown in this rib repair drawing... *(deHMC)*

LEFT: ...and this spar repair drawing. *(deHMC)*

BELOW: Small areas of damage or elongated holes can often be repaired with packing blocks. *(Arthur Mason)*

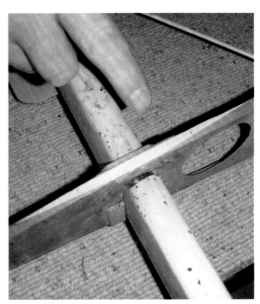

in smaller components such as the wing ribs and similar structures. While the bigger components lent themselves to mechanised production, the creation of the wing ribs was a hugely labour-intensive operation. No less than 48 are required for each aeroplane, every one assembled from over 30 individual small pieces of wood. During the war this had the advantage of enabling small offcuts from larger components to be usefully recycled.

Wood repairs

For restorers brought up on balsa-wood model aircraft the process of wood repairs will already be familiar. Repairing a Tiger Moth is the same only on a bigger scale! Provided that damage has not occurred within 600mm of a major load-bearing point, such as the wing-root ends or interplane strut mountings, even major components such as the wing spars can often be repaired rather than replaced. Approved repair schemes will allow ash packing blocks to be used to repair small areas of damage or elongated bolt holes. For bigger repairs, new wood can be added in the form of a scarf joint, in which old and new pieces are equally tapered over a precise length in accord with the wood grain. Properly made this will be as strong as, if not stronger than the original wood.

The angle of the scarf joint is critical to its strength. For major load-bearing components an angle of 1 in 20 is normally required. Therefore to replace a piece of wood 10mm deep, the length of the joint will be 200mm, giving an adhesive area of 20cm^2. The accurate cutting of the joint is achieved by means of a smoothing plane set to its finest setting. A coarse setting will chip the wood and create a poor jointing surface.

After marking out the scarf using a rule, pencil and carpenter's square, the joint is initially roughly cut using a tenon saw, before the timber is secured to the workbench by G-clamps and scrapwood blocks, with the longest edge of the scarf lowermost. The joint face should also be supported by a piece of scrap wood with a straight edge, clamped below the edge to be planed so as to prevent the timber bending and causing an inaccurate joint angle.

During the planing, regular checks are made to ensure that the joint surface is level and true. Once both pieces of timber have been planed they are carefully matched to ensure that they will match. Then adhesive is applied and the joint is clamped to cure.

The glue originally used for wooden components on the Tiger Moth was a casein-based adhesive, made of proteins from milk products. However, it proved prone to moisture and bacterial damage and modern repairs are generally made using resorcinol glues such as Aerodux.

The glue is applied to both surfaces of the joint, which are then rubbed together to exclude any air bubbles before the timbers are clamped in place, sandwiched between two pieces of scrap wood longer than the joint in order to spread the load. The G-clamps should exert adequate but not excessive force. Strips of waxed paper or cling film should be used to prevent glue adhering to the packing blocks and clamps should never be used directly on the aircraft timber due to the risk of compression damage.

Once the glue has set, the packing strips are removed and, if properly executed, the joint will need only light sanding to remove surplus adhesive. Not only does another piece of Tiger Moth live to fly again, but the pleasure of having hand-crafted the component from wood, nature's composite, is far greater than could ever be attained using a modern carbon-fibre equivalent.

Fabric repairs

In the rough and tumble world of elementary flying training, the Tiger Moth's fabric-covered structure proved easy and quick to repair. Where a metal-skinned aeroplane requiring a replacement panel could be unserviceable for days, minor damage to a Tiger Moth's covering could be rapidly repaired and the aeroplane swiftly returned to service.

The most likely areas of damage, both then and now, are to the lower wingtips or ailerons, the tail covering as a result of stones or debris,

The repair process shown in this 1938 manual remains exactly the same as that used today.

The old dope and paint is first removed from the area and the fabric is stitched back together. The area around the patch is redoped and the doped patch placed over the tear. *(Newnes Manual)*

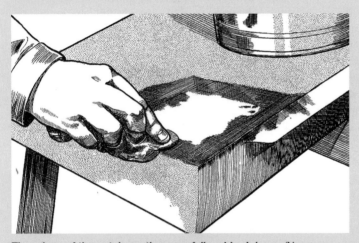

The edges of the patch are then carefully rubbed down. *(Newnes Manual)*

When dry the whole patch is redoped. *(Newnes Manual)*

and the lower wing fabric if someone has inadvertently taxied over an object such as a marker board. In every case the first priority is to rigorously check that no further structural damage has been caused.

Damage to the wingtips after touching the ground in a landing incident may, for example, point to the risk of structural damage to the wing spars at their fuselage mountings due to the leverage applied along the wing structure. Wrinkling of the fabric at the fuselage may also indicate damage to the longerons. In either case a full structural inspection is required.

Assuming that the damage is localised and minor, the fabric around the tear is cleaned up and any loose strands removed before the area is prepared by removing the existing dope using an approved solvent. Acetate dopes are effectively a suspension of microscopic wood fibres in an acetone solution, therefore neat acetone will remove the old dope and leave the fabric ready to act as a base for the repair.

In recent years many aircraft have been re-covered with more modern fabrics, butyrate dopes and polyurethane-based paint finishes. In these cases, the surface of the finish is lightly sanded to provide a key for the new dope, to eliminate the risk of reaction between the different materials.

With traditional cotton or linen, the prepared fabric surrounding the tear is brushed with new dope before a prepared patch of similar material is thoroughly doped, laid over the tear and smoothed down with either a firm doping brush or a wad of doped fabric. Modern synthetic fabrics can be shrunk by heat from an iron, before finishing dope is applied. The patch, which is slightly larger than the area of damage, is cut with pinking shears to give a serrated edge which resists fraying.

Once the repaired panel has cured, becoming hard and dry, the patch is doped a second time. When this second coat is dry a final finish of pigmented dope or matching paint may be applied, and the aeroplane is once again ready to go. Of course, any such work must be supervised by a certified engineer or maintenance organisation and conform to their maintenance and sign-off procedures.

A phoenix from the ashes

The aeroplane featured in many of the pictures in this section, G-ACDA, is a historic machine in its own right. It was the first of the new and upgraded DH82A types to be built, completed at the de Havilland factory at Stag Lane, Edgware, in February 1933. However, that is only a part of the story. Its rise from the ashes – literally – is little short of amazing.

After spending its initial years with the de Havilland School of Flying at Hatfield, the aeroplane was impressed into military service in 1940. By 1943, being then ten years old, it was considered too elderly for continued service so was 'pensioned off', being sold to a Devon landowner and stored in a barn near Exeter. For most redundant aeroplanes at the height of World War Two, that would have spelt the end. But in this case it was just the beginning of the story.

The aeroplane was rediscovered in 1972 by the Secretary of the Exeter Flying Club, Richard Biddle, and in June 1979 it flew again, appropriately from its wartime base of Kemble in Gloucestershire. However, just a few weeks later disaster struck when the aircraft struck an electricity pylon. Thankfully both the pilot and Biddle, who was passenger on his first and only flight in six years of ownership, escaped. The aeroplane, though, was consumed in the ensuing fire.

Undaunted, restoration was commenced for a second time. Amazingly, while the wooden structures of the wings and tail unit were turned to ashes, the angle at which the wreckage had been suspended from the electricity pylon meant that the steel-tube fuselage and

the engine had survived. There was even fuel remaining in an undamaged tank! The aeroplane began to take shape again, only to suffer the disappearance of many of its major components. At this point, Richard Biddle sadly decided that enough was enough.

Once again, though, the aeroplane refused to die. The project was acquired in 1997 by Bryn Hughes, who worked with Jan Cooper and the Newbury Aeroplane Company to complete a stunning restoration to the aeroplane's original pre-WW2 condition. Phoenix-like, G-ACDA rose from the ashes in 2008, and today flies from one of the RAF's last all-grass airfields, at Henlow in Bedfordshire.

'As I fly, looking down on the English countryside, I feel a bond with generations past. It's a very special feeling which you only get with a Tiger Moth.'

Cathy Silk
Tiger Moth owner

Chapter Three

The owner's view

Owning and enjoying a Tiger Moth

While the days of the mythical 'ten-pound Tiger', surplus from military service, have long since passed, the dream of owning and flying a Tiger Moth is still fulfilled by many people around the world.

Of 8,800 built, the records at the de Havilland Moth Club indicate that around 1,100 Tiger Moth identities can still be traced worldwide. Of these, over half remain airworthy and the vast majority are owned and enjoyed by private individuals.

LEFT: The joys of owning a Tiger Moth are as timeless as the aeroplane itself. *(Andy Smith)*

The timeless sight of
a Tiger Moth over the
English countryside on
a summer's afternoon.
(Andy Smith)

Today there are many routes to sampling the Tiger Moth experience. They range from trial flying lessons and 'joy-rides' with established operators, to more extended pilot training with flying clubs, syndicate or shared group-ownership, and – the ultimate pleasure – owning a Tiger Moth of one's own.

The Tiger Moth is not without its critics. Aviation writer and aerobatics ace Brian Lecomber once described it as 'a wonderful nostalgic flying device, but it will never replace the aeroplane'. He went on to question the judgement of anyone prepared to exchange a comfortable, heated, enclosed cockpit for one having 'all the creature comforts of a medieval ducking-stool'. Yet even he acknowledges that the Tiger Moth exudes 'vintage charm', and it is this charm, along with the challenges and pleasures presented to pilot and passenger alike, that ensures a continuing demand for these aircraft.

Although prices inevitably vary around the world, in Great Britain the going price for a good airworthy example is currently around £40–50,000. This is comparable to a valuable classic car and therefore within the means of a wealthy individual enthusiast.

However, a Tiger Moth requires more than money, it also soaks up time. Any vintage aeroplane, whether flown or not, demands continuous, time-consuming maintenance to avoid a steady decline in condition. For this reason many Tiger Moths are owned by 'groups' or small syndicates of up to a dozen individuals who share running costs and maintenance tasks. The operation of these small enthusiastic groups also serves an important 'self-assessment' role, as the members continually monitor one-another's flying performance, share experiences and plan flights together that perhaps a less experienced pilot would not attempt on their own. They are a great way to learn about Moths.

Most flying groups require a new member to first pay a lump sum to purchase a share of the aeroplane from an outgoing owner. These are sometimes advertised in the specialist pilots' magazines, more often in *The Moth*, the quarterly publication of the de Havilland Moth Club; but it is equally likely that the recommendation will come by word of mouth.

On at least one occasion an offer of assistance in pushing an aeroplane out of the hangar has resulted first in an offer of a flight in a spare seat, followed by a chat in the bar, and has ended a few months later with the volunteer becoming a part-owner!

Within a syndicate, the costs are shared among all members in the form of fixed monthly charges, plus an additional charge for each hour flown. The monthly charges cover hangarage and airfield fees, the costs of annual inspections and routine maintenance, insurance, and normally a contribution to an 'engine fund' or similar in anticipation of future maintenance. If other repairs or maintenance are required each member pays their share of the bill.

These costs inevitably vary from syndicate to syndicate, not least based on the aircraft's location. For example, all Tiger Moths require

ABOVE: This aeroplane, G-ANFM, is owned by a syndicate of 12 members, who share the costs and fun! They have operated the same aeroplane for 40 years, making them the longest-established such group in the UK. *(Geoff Collins)*

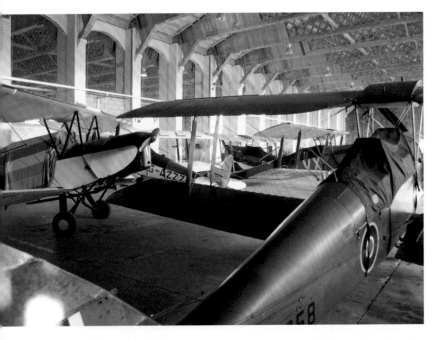

ABOVE: Indoor hangarage is a must if the condition of the aeroplane is not to deteriorate markedly. At Henlow, a number of Moths enjoy both an all-grass airfield and residence in a historic 'Belfast Truss' hangar dating back to World War One. *(Geoff Collins)*

BELOW: Companies operating 'Tiger Moth experience' flights around the world enable young and old alike to enjoy classic open-cockpit flying. *(Malcolm Ward, via Geoff Collins)*

OPPOSITE TOP: Suitably trained, volunteers can get *very* close to the action. For example, someone has to hold the poles for the aerial limbo competition! *(Geoff Collins)*

OPPOSITE BOTTOM: Being involved with Tiger Moths sometimes gains you access to very exclusive events, such as this invitation-only picnic in the grounds of Houghton Hall in Norfolk. *(Geoff Collins)*

indoor hangarage if their condition is not to deteriorate rapidly, but even if a space can be found at a busy general aviation airfield on the outskirts of a major city like London the cost of this will be several thousand pounds a year. Therefore many Tiger Moths operate from smaller airfields or private airstrips on farms, where hangarage may be the corner of a barn but flying is significantly cheaper and delightfully less regulated.

Of course, one does not have to be a Moth owner to savour the experience. In Great Britain, America, Australia, New Zealand and South Africa, as well as other locations around the world, established operators offer trial flights in Tiger Moths over an amazing range of scenery.

Whether it is the Canadian Prairies, the 'Lord of the Rings' landscape of New Zealand, the beaches of Australia's Gold Coast, the interlocked meadows of Great Britain or following in the footsteps of *Out of Africa* legends Denys Finch-Hatton and Beryl Markham on an elephant-spotting Tiger Moth safari, something special is added to any view when it is framed by the wings and wires of a vintage biplane.

Even if one is not interested in one's feet leaving the ground, there are plenty of opportunities to get 'up close and personal' with Tiger Moths.

Membership of the de Havilland Moth Club is open not just to owners and pilots, but to anyone with an interest in the classic aeroplanes designed and built by the de Havilland Aircraft Company. As a member, one will be invited to assist at air shows and charity flying events as well as other club activities. A willing team known as the 'Mainwaring Volunteer Force' is a vital part of deHMC activities.

Other organisations too, such as the Shuttleworth Vintage Aviation Society in the UK, the New Zealand Sport and Vintage Aviation Society and the Collingwood Classic Aircraft Foundation in Canada, all encourage volunteers to assist keeping their aeroplanes flying.

A unique training record

The unbroken record of one organisation in training pilots on Tiger Moths is unique. This is the Cambridge Flying Group, formed as far back as 1953 by three enthusiasts, who appointed Bill Ison, an instructor in the RAF Reserve, as Chief Flying Instructor.

Bill has shared his wealth of experience with several hundreds, if not thousands, of students to date. While it would be indelicate to discuss Bill's age, he will admit that not too long from now it will be 80 years since he made his first flight from Cambridge, as a small boy, in a DH60 Moth. His 20-minute flight cost his mother 2s 6d (12½p) and sparked an infectious enthusiasm for flying, teaching and Tiger Moths that remains undiminished.

The Cambridge Flying Group is not a staffed flying school in the normal sense. It is run via a committee and has a membership of around 100, of whom 70 are flying members. On average ten pilots at a time are training for their Private Pilot's Licence, with instruction given by fully qualified volunteer flying instructors. The group owns two DH82a Tiger Moths, G-AOEI and G-AHIZ, and has its own dispersal area, hangar and small clubhouse at Cambridge Airport.

While the Cambridge Flying Group's longevity makes it unique, other flying schools also continue to operate Tiger Moths to complement fleets of more modern aircraft. The fact that there is a demand to be fulfilled is testament to the Tiger Moth's most enduring legacy. It continues to charm and challenge pilots in equal measure.

Flying for fun

While the Tiger Moth was devised with a serious training role in mind, even the worst of the wartime years could not diminish the feelings of pleasure, euphoria and achievement that came with one's first flight in a Tiger Moth. In the post-war years continuing affection for the type, combined initially with low cost and availability, made it the aircraft of choice for many whose aim was simply to fly for the sake of flying.

Then as now for most such pilots, an evening 'bimble' flying a friend over their house, or a Sunday afternoon trip to a nearby airfield, was sufficient. Others sought to extend their flying skills ever further, with precision formation flying, air racing, competition aerobatics and even floatplane flying. Many of these pilots gravitated to the Tiger Club, which developed some spectacular variations on the Tiger Moth theme.

Super Tigers

Four specially modified Tiger Moths were created by the Tiger Club to participate in competition aerobatic events. They featured a more powerful Gipsy Major 1C engine and a modified fuel system which allowed the engine to continue to develop power while in inverted flight.

One obvious visual feature of these aeroplanes was the removal of the fuel tank from the upper wing and its installation in the faired-over front cockpit, turning the aeroplane into a single-seater. Their enhanced performance allowed pilots such as Neil Williams, Colin Labouchere and Barry Tempest to represent Britain against Zlin, Stampe and Bucker designs in international aerobatic competitions.

The first of these 'Super Tigers' was named 'The Bishop', in tribute to the Tiger Club's Chief Flying Instructor, C. Nepean Bishop. 'When the second one was built, a few of us younger members of the club wanted to name it "The Actress",' says Tiger Moth aerobatic ace Barry Tempest. 'But things were a bit more straight-laced in those days. Ultimately the other three were named "The Archbishop", "The Canon" and "The Deacon".

'One key to enjoying your Tiger Moth is to only fly in the summer months. And then, only fly when the air temperature is higher than 20°C,' jokes Barry. 'Incipient hypothermia can blunt your enjoyment in about 20 minutes flat!'

Barry in fact has plenty of experience in flying Tiger Moths in all temperatures, weathers and attitudes. He learned to fly Tiger Moths in a small private flying group in Norfolk in 1957 and half a century later had amassed some 13,000 flying hours on light aeroplanes. Of these, over 2,000 have been flown in Tiger Moths, initially as a pupil, then as private pilot, instructor and

one of the type's most highly regarded display pilots.

'We were very lucky, in that initially the instructors in the flying group where I learned were from a World War Two military background, and their high standards and professional style contributed a great deal to our formative years. Everyone was a volunteer, we operated off a former RAF base and we kept the costs to an absolute minimum. Back in 1957 our hourly flying rate was £1.25 per hour. It only rose to about £3 per hour over the next ten years.'

Today those low prices are long gone. Most owners budget at least £150 per flying hour, yet Barry applies the same simple formula of 'getting the maximum smiles per gallon', or 'laughs per litre', from Tiger Moth flying.

'The most important factor in my opinion is to increase your personal flying skills in what is now very much a vintage aeroplane,' says Barry. 'Many aspects necessary for competence in aircraft like ours are neglected in modern

BELOW: Whether it is practising formation flying, or perfecting the seamless spot landing, Barry Tempest's answer to getting fun from the Tiger Moth for over 50 years is to never stop learning. *(Geoff Collins)*

pilot training. They're largely irrelevant with present-day production light aeroplanes. These include taildragger handling, side-slipping and, perhaps most vitally, the need to use rudder to co-ordinate aileron application. A joy of flying and of the Tiger Moth is that you simply never stop learning.'

A loop and a roll on a Sunday afternoon

While some private pilots practice aerobatics with a view to displaying an aeroplane or entering competitions, the majority prefer to hone their skills simply for fun and as a means of raising their standards of airmanship. Barry Tempest describes this as 'LAROSA' flying – 'A Loop and a Roll On Sunday Afternoon', in which the Tiger Moth continues to demonstrate surprising agility.

'The Tiger Moth is a nice vintage aerobatic machine,' says Barry. 'But you have to fly it within limitations that don't necessarily apply to more modern or exotic types. You start off with a limited amount of potential energy in the form of height, and inevitably in the Tiger you expend that energy by getting lower and lower as the sequence proceeds.'

Barry's typical aerobatic sequence will begin with a diving approach to a loop, followed by a barrel roll then a chandelle, a steep climbing wingover to recover momentum and reverse the direction of flight. Another favoured manoeuvre is a Cuban Eight, which involves a five-eighths of a loop, followed by a half-roll on a diving 45° line. The manoeuvre is then repeated to create a horizontal figure-of-eight in the sky.

BELOW: Barry Tempest practices competition aerobatics in a 'Barnstormers' Tiger Moth in the 1960s. *(Matthew Boddington)*

However, there are some manoeuvres for which the Tiger Moth is less than suitable. The fact that it has ailerons only on the bottom wings means that the standard aileron roll is at best ponderous.

While flick rolls were possible with the Super Tiger Moths, using elevator and rudder to snap the aeroplane around its axis in a semi-stalled condition, Barry advises against attempting them in standard Tigers, as they generate significant stress on what is now an aged airframe.

'The Tiger Moth simply doesn't impress with rolling manoeuvres anyway. A modern aerobatic biplane like the Pitts Special will complete about six rolls in the time it takes a Tiger to roll once,' says Barry. 'I love the Tiger Moth and you can have a lot of fun with aerobatics in it, but you fly it within its limits.'

Putting on a show

So, what makes a good Tiger Moth display? Although an award-winning aerobatics pilot, Barry Tempest doesn't necessarily believe that a Tiger Moth needs to be flown in high-energy aerobatics to show it to best effect.

'Most Tiger Moth airframes are older than I am, and these days I don't subject myself to extreme G-forces. I see no reason to subject a similarly old aeroplane to them either,' he says. 'The Tiger Moth is one of the most versatile display aeroplanes. It can be used in so many different types of act.

'The aim of any display is to show your aircraft off to the audience without in any way getting close to the limits of either pilot or aeroplane. The simplest type of non-aerobatic "flypast" display is in fact very effective in showing off the aeroplane in its best light.

'Take-off, make a "dumb-bell" turn to bring you back onto the crowd line at 100ft,' suggests Barry. 'A fast run down-wind is followed by another dumb-bell turn for a slower run into the wind, accelerating into a 360° turn to let photographers see the topside of the aeroplane.

'Another dumb-bell turn for a final fast run downwind then a last dumb-bell turn to position you for a side-slipping, curved approach to land. That will take five minutes and show off all the best aspects of the aeroplane. I'm a firm believer of the KISS principle – keep it simple.'

However, Barry advises strongly against any pilot attempting an ad hoc display, for example at a local garden fete. Not only is it hazardous, in the UK any such display is illegal unless written permission has been obtained from the Civil Aviation Authority. To gain this approval the aircraft must carry additional third-party display insurance and the pilot must demonstrate that the display has been fully rehearsed and signed off with a written Display Authorisation from a CAA-appointed evaluator.

Barnstorming

One of the pioneers of exciting air display acts performed with vintage biplanes was Lewis Benjamin, known throughout the Moth world as 'Benjy'.

BELOW: A pretty girl on the upper wing is, of course, a key part of the show. Being lighter, it also helps the Tiger Moth's marginal performance with the added drag of the wing-walker! *(Matthew Boddington)*

A former fighter pilot and RAF Volunteer Reserve member, Benjy was one of the earliest members of the Tiger Club when it was formed in 1957. As with all its members he was encouraged to push the envelope of his flying skill in air shows and barnstorming acts with Tiger Moths throughout the 1960s.

In that period, Benjy perhaps claimed two specific claims to notoriety. The first came when he suggested that to spice up the air show routine someone should stand on the top wing in flight.

Not surprisingly it took nearly three years to devise a scheme which satisfied the aviation authorities, but in March 1962 Benjy became the first aviator in modern times to experience flight from this new viewpoint. Today the 'stand-on-wing' routine he pioneered has been elevated to new levels by the Guinot wing-walking formation team, as well as other display teams around the world, but Benjy, on a Tiger Moth, was the pioneer.

He added spice less intentionally to another Tiger Club air show in 1963, when, during a low-level crazy-flying display, his aircraft flicked into a spin and dived vertically into the ground.

Amazingly Benjy was lifted from the wreckage with just a broken nose, bloodshot eye and bruised leg. He and the Tiger Moth were both flying again before the season was out!

Captain Neville's Flying Circus

Today the most spectacular barnstorming-type Tiger Moth display is carried out by 'Captain Neville's Flying Circus'. It sees a cavalcade of classic types – including Tiger Moths, a rare Jackaroo derivative, Chipmunks and others – carrying out 'limbo' acts, bursting balloons, flour-bombing targets, cutting streamers and picking up ribbons with wingtips.

The leader of the team, Dennis Neville, made his first passenger flight in an Auster from Christchurch, Dorset, in 1960. Says Dennis: 'The landing was so bad I decided to find out if I could do better.'

He joined the Air Training Corps and went solo in a glider at RAF Swanton Morley in 1962, then joined the de Havilland Engine Company as an apprentice. Later, whilst in the Army as an Aircraft Technician, he went solo again in a de Havilland Chipmunk at RAF Seletar and gained his Private Pilot's Licence whilst in Singapore in 1970.

Since then he has flown as a gliding instructor, crop-sprayer, air taxi and night freight pilot, and commanded airliners and corporate jets. Today his logbook contains over 14,500 hours of flying, on more than 90 types ranging from Sopwith Dove to Hunter jet fighter.

Now retired from flying 'heavy metal', Dennis and his wife Tricia form the centrepiece of the Flying Circus. Their traditional barnstorming style enlivens air shows around the UK and places a firm emphasis on precision flying and good airmanship, rather than high-energy manoeuvres.

The 'limbo' routine, for example, requires the pilot to fly his or her aeroplane under a row of ribbons, held aloft on 5m poles set just a few metres further apart than a Tiger Moth's wingspan. To pass safely beneath, the Tiger Moth's wheels should be just half a metre above the ground!

BELOW: Aerial limbo flying demands precision and accurate timing, and is a great test of airmanship. Points are deducted if a pilot climbs above the bunting, or the aircraft wheels touch the ground.
(Geoff Collins)

Long-haul Tigers

The slow cruising speed and limited endurance of a Tiger Moth should, theoretically, mitigate against the type being used for long-distance flights. However, that doesn't account for the ability of Tiger Moth owners to rise to the challenge.

In 1978, David Cyster – at the time a fighter pilot with the RAF – decided to celebrate the Australian pilot Bert Hinckler's record-breaking 1928 flight from Croydon to Sydney. Cyster's mount was his 1941-built Tiger Moth, G-ANRF, modified with long-distance fuel tanks that enabled it to remain airborne for more than ten hours at a time.

Cyster's route took him from Dunsfold in Surrey to Marseilles, then along the northern edge of the Mediterranean, across Egypt and the Gulf States, Pakistan, India, Burma, Thailand, Malaysia, Singapore and Indonesia. Five weeks later the Tiger Moth touched down in Darwin in Northern Australia before continuing at a more leisurely pace to arrive to a hero's welcome in Sydney.

Cyster still owns and enjoys his faithful Tiger Moth, which was reconverted to two-seat specification after returning (by ship) from Australia, but while a select number of Tiger Moth owners have followed in his path by flying from England to Australia, so far only one Tiger Moth flight has achieved the feat from East to West. Barry Markham's flight from Australia to England was against all the prevailing winds, giving an average ground speed of just 60mph (100kph).

As Barry lives in Cambridge, Western Australia, and had also flown Tiger Moths with the Cambridge Flying Group in the UK, the start and finish points were clearly defined. As Barry has chronicled his adventure in his book *Solo to England*, we'll omit the details of his 172 airborne hours. Suffice to say that he and 'Margery' the Tiger Moth made it, testament to aeroplane and aviator alike.

Another Tiger Moth and owner partnership that revels in the challenges of long-distance travel is G-ANRN and Jonathan Elwes. In 1989 Jonathan decided to celebrate *Glasnost*

and the warming of relations between Britain and Russia by a flight to Moscow. His Tiger Moth, nicknamed 'Glasmoth', led a formation of three Tigers, and in the company of Nick Parkhouse, Roger Fiennes and three Russian navigators made the round trip in a total of 20 days.

However, that was just the start for Elwes. In 1994 he and his Tiger made an equally epic trip to the Arctic Circle, flying round the North Cape. Then in 2005 he flew the biplane across Eastern Europe to Ukraine. His destination was the Crimea and Balaclava, to recreate the 'Charge of the Light Brigade'. Elwes flew his Tiger Moth down the line of the cavalry charge with the standards of the 11th Hussars and the 4th Light Dragoons flying from each wing strut!

ABOVE: Where to next? DH Tiger Moth owners' long-distance travels continue to amaze. *(Geoff Collins)*

BELOW: Jonathan Elwes (seen here filtering fuel with the aid of a chamois leather) has made several long-distance tours, including one to Moscow and to Balaclava in the Crimea, to fly the course of the Charge of the Light Brigade. *(Jonathan Elwes via deHMC)*

ABOVE: Led by Jeff
Milsom, 11 Tiger
Moths and 13 pilots
each year give up their
time to practice and
then to display as the
Tiger Nine formation
team. (Geoff Collins)

Tiger Nine

Perhaps the best-known Tiger Moths are
those which have flown over the years with
the Diamond Nine and Tiger Nine teams.
Over the past two decades they have been
unique in offering the sight and sound of nine
vintage biplanes flying in tight formation.

The displays were inspired by pre-war
formation flying by Tiger Moths of the Central
Flying School, and the Diamond Nine Team
was formed in 1986 by Tiger Moth owner
Charles Shea-Simmons. He recruited a team
of like-minded owners, all unpaid volunteers,
and for more than a decade wowed the
crowds at major air shows in the United
Kingdom and overseas.

However, to quote Shea-Simmons,
'the advancing ages of both aeroplanes
and pilots', along with the pressures of
maintaining a team of nine independently-
owned aeroplanes meant that the end of

the 2000 air display season marked the final
display by Diamond Nine. It seemed as if an
era had come to an end, until 2005, when
Tiger Moth owner Jeff Milsom responded to
a request for a flypast of nine Tiger Moths
at the 25th de Havilland Moth Club rally at
Woburn Abbey.

Formed around a core of former Diamond
Nine members, the new team led by Jeff
began the series of practice sessions
necessary to achieve a safely-flown, large,
close formation flypast. Once they'd achieved
the necessary level of competence, it seemed a
pity not to continue!

The Tiger Nine team is currently drawn
from a core of 11 aircraft and 12 pilots from
a wide variety of backgrounds. They include
ex-RAF pilots, airline captains, a farmer, a
sales executive, a company director, an air
ambulance specialist, an anaesthetist and an
RAF Wing Commander, flying a limited number

of displays each year in support of the de Havilland Moth Club.

An important aspect of the Tiger Nine team's structure is its ability to invite new members and train them to be part of the team. Prospective new members are invited early each year to attend training sessions which concentrate on the basics of close formation. Flown dual initially, in a formation of two of three, these cover joining, keeping position, dismantling the formation, safety and emergencies.

Later each spring the team meet for three main practice days, at a private field in rural Wiltshire where they enjoy relatively clear airspace and no circuit traffic. Starting with formations of three or four to refresh formation flying skills, each practice concludes with a flypast and bomb burst for that section of the larger formation. The first day concludes with all sections flying together for the first time in a nine-ship display.

The Tiger Moth is a surprisingly challenging machine for a formation display. Its sluggish aileron control and relatively low power are combined with a light wing loading and low flying speed, which makes the formation prone to air turbulence.

On occasion it is not unusual to see the entire formation execute a 'wave' as first the leading aircraft strikes a rising air current and surges upwards, to be followed in turn by the rest of the team. For many spectators it is a key part of the charm of the display.

For the pilots, Tiger Nine is described as 'real flying', meaning fun enhanced by the camaraderie of a great group of like-minded people. And that is what Tiger Moth ownership is all about.

Buying a Tiger

There can be few aeroplanes that are simpler or stronger than a Tiger Moth. Equally, however, there are few aeroplanes left flying which will have had such a long or hard-working life. Only rarely does a genuine, unmolested, ex-service airframe come to light, and even then it was probably rebuilt several times during its war service.

Over the decades of any Tiger Moth's life most will have had new engines, wings and even fuselage sections fitted. Just like the original road-sweeper's broom, it has been in service for decades with regular changes of head and handle.

A scan of the pages of magazines such as the de Havilland Moth Club members' quarterly *The Moth* will reveal a wide range of aircraft, from immaculate show-winning restorations by established restorers to a collection of tubes and timber in the back of a barn or even an attic.

Most buyers, of course, opt for a more median course, and seek an aircraft that is not immaculate but is sound and airworthy, although plenty of projects are available to tempt the more adventurous. A general rule of thumb is that it is better to buy a sound flyable example for £40,000 than a basket case for £20,000 and then have to spend upwards of £35–40,000 to get it flying.

While the acquisition of a Tiger Moth is feasible for a committed individual, it certainly isn't the cheapest way to enter sport aviation. A classic two-seat light aircraft such as a Jodel can be purchased in the UK for around £15,000. The same money would probably buy a worn but basically serviceable ex-flying club Cessna or Piper. Or you could just about buy an abandoned Tiger Moth rebuild project or an insurance write-off.

To acquire a basically complete aircraft in long-term storage, with the relevant logbooks and documentation to allow a 'recommissioning' to airworthiness, the minimum price in the UK will be around £25,000.

A price of around £30–40,000 will be sought for a complete flying aircraft in 'tired' condition. It probably has high engine hours and will almost certainly require some work at the time of its next annual or certificate of airworthiness inspection.

The majority of Tiger Moths, however, are offered in the bracket of £40–50,000 at the time of writing. Most will have had a fairly recent engine overhaul and will have a generally clean airframe. The higher the standard of restoration, the higher will be the price. As can be imagined, for a truly immaculate, 'as new' example with details such as perfectly restored original instrumentation, the sky can be the limit!

An inspection of the airframe and engine logbooks – the vital first step in any purchase – should show the engineers' signatures for all routine maintenance.

All mandatory modifications specified in the engine and airframe Technical News Sheets should also have been complied with and signed-off in the logbooks. There should be information too on any items which may have been given a mandatory 'life' by the airworthiness authorities.

Engine

The cost of engine rebuilds is generally greater than that of airframe work, therefore a rule of thumb is that a good engine in a tatty airframe is better than the other way round. Within the many Gipsy Major permutations the later 1C model with aluminium cylinder heads has both more power and a longer valve-seat life with modern high-octane fuels than the earlier bronze-headed versions.

Ensuring that the aeroplane is chocked, and treating the propeller as always, of course, as if the ignition is live – even if the four magneto switches are down for 'off' – pull the engine through compressions four times. The four compressions should be even. If they are not, suspect either the valves or piston rings in one cylinder. An engineer's differential compression test will quickly tell you which area to check further.

A final simple test as one pulls the propeller through compression is to put a chair or stool so that the propeller blade tip just brushes past it. Now see if the second blade tracks behind the other. If not, the propeller isn't tracking correctly. At a minimum this may mean sloppy maintenance, at worst crankshaft run-out after someone has bent it wrecking an earlier propeller. Also look for cracks in the wooden propeller itself, excessive wear, and indications of movement at the hub.

Ask the owner to start the engine for a ground run, and when it fires check how long it takes for the oil pressure to rise. It should rise within around 10–15 seconds and once the engine has warmed up should sit at around 35–40psi at normal running speeds.

One can assume all is well if the engine starts well, holds oil pressure, runs smoothly at idle and under load, and doesn't throw out clouds of smoke. After shutting down make a final inspection of the crankcase for hairline cracks near the cylinder bases or any other significant oil leaks, check the throttle connections for excessive play, blowing exhaust gaskets and traces of the blue dye which is placed in aviation fuel to highlight any fuel or carburettor leaks.

One piece of possible future legislation which may need to be borne in mind is the number of years since the engine was last overhauled. A recent failure of a Gipsy Major engine which had flown a very low number of hours, but had been in storage for more than a decade, may, for aircraft which carry a public transport Certificate of Airworthiness, prompt a mandatory inspection of the crankshaft for corrosion every ten years. While this will not unduly affect more recently rebuilt engines, or aircraft used solely for private use, an older engine – even if it has only been lightly utilised – may need to be stripped.

Airframe

If you are looking at a complete aircraft, begin your inspection from about 20m away. Are the wings level? If they are not, is this caused by wear in the undercarriage components, flat tyres, or a more serious problem with the aircraft rigging?

If it is a rigging or wing structure issue, any slackness or over-tension in the cabane, incidence, landing and flying wires may indicate damage, neglect or unskilled maintenance.

The wooden areas of the airframe all require inspection to check for damage, rot or glue failure. In 1998 a mandatory inspection (TNS32) was required of the wooden wing structures of all Tiger Moths. In many cases this necessitated the cutting of inspection holes in the aircraft's fabric, with patches being subsequently doped in place. A check in the logbooks should confirm that this has been carried out.

In addition to visual inspection, as soon as an inspection panel is removed sniff the inside of the wing. A musty smell is an early warning of dampness, mould or rot. You should also gently press with your fingers on the wooden structures of the wing, wing walkways, fuselage decking and tail surfaces for signs of broken ribs, rot or glue failure.

The overall condition of the fabric covering should be evaluated too. Just dismantling and re-rigging a Tiger Moth costs around £3,000, and if the fabric needs replacing re-covering will cost more than £10,000 and painting almost the same again.

Finally you must check the fuselage, steel undercarriage, tail-bracing and cabane struts for signs of damage, corrosion and general integrity. There is a mandatory schedule (TNS29) for the replacement of the tie rods which brace the fuselage structure at the lower wing mountings. This restricts the components to a service life of 2,000 flying hours or 18 years, whichever is sooner. It is also mandatory to examine the structure following a heavy landing and at every annual inspection.

If an aeroplane has been poorly stored the rear fuselage frame tubes are sometimes corroded from the inside due to water ingress or condensation. If the tubes sound dull when tapped, or you can hear or feel rust flakes, the fuselage may have to be stripped and inspected.

Check the fixtures and fittings. Are the instruments working and is there a full, matching set in both cockpits? Seats should be checked for cracks and loose mountings. A little play in the controls can be expected, but they shouldn't be sloppy or loose-fitting. Harnesses too should be in good condition, and if the traditional 'Sutton' type is used they should be checked to ensure that they haven't exceeded their service life.

Finally, check the aluminium cowlings and oil tank for fatigue cracks near their fittings, and inspect and check that the fuel tank, pipes and on-off tap aren't leaking. Control cables where accessible should be checked for condition and fraying.

While the checks above sound daunting, they are not exhaustive and the presence of a suitably qualified engineer is highly recommended at any pre-purchase inspection. The good news is that the majority of Tiger Moths are prized, well maintained and ready to give their owners many years of service.

All-weather adventure

While most Tiger Moth owners save their flying for calm, warm summer days, there are, as you might expect, exceptions to the rule.

Bruno Vonlanthen is the Chairman of the Moth Club of Switzerland and the proud owner of both a Tiger Moth and a de Havilland Moth Major. Each year for the past decade, he and his Tiger Moth, HB-UBC, have taken part in a unique fly-in to the frozen lake of Schwarzsee, high in the Alps. Their destination requires a landing on ice, 3,400ft (1,000m) above sea level.

'Frozen lakes have always been used in Switzerland, they are one of the few flat areas we have got,' jokes Bruno. 'Moth owners used frozen lakes in places like Saint Moritz and Schwarzsee in the 1930s, but now this is the last airfield of its kind. Open, weather permitting, just two days a year.

'I pre-heat the engine with a heater under a blanket and warm the oil in a pan before starting, but the old girl has no big problems with the cold,' says Vonlanthen, an engineer with the Swiss Air Force. 'I pay special attention to preparation, warm clothes, good goggles with no air gaps, and I warm up with a cup of tea before flying, more tea and hot sausages when I arrive. The only problem is my modern radio. The microphone sometimes freezes and stops working!'

'The challenge of making the perfect landing stays with you as long as you fly Tiger Moths, adding spice to every flight.'

Nick Bloom
Pilot Magazine

Chapter Four

The pilot's view

Taming the Tiger

When it was new the de Havilland Tiger Moth was regarded as 'relatively easy to fly, but difficult to fly well'. For a pilot brought up on more modern machinery, it requires a complete change of mindset. There are no compromises. The Tiger Moth was designed in the 1930s and still requires the skills of that era, and before, in order to be operated safely today.

LEFT: The Tiger Moth was designed when airfields had no marked runways. Instead, one simply landed into wind. *(Geoff Collins)*

Nick Bloom is editor of *Pilot Magazine*, and in the course of his occupation flies the widest range of aeroplanes, ancient and modern. His objective look at flying in a Tiger Moth, as seen through the eyes of a modern light aircraft pilot, first appeared in *Pilot Magazine* in November 2004:

'The Tiger Moth isn't everyone's cup of tea. Maintenance devours time and money. You have to swing the propeller by hand to start the engine, with the attendant risks to life and limb.

'In flight, it is slow, noisy, draughty, difficult to land and vulnerable to crosswinds. Unless the engine has been recently overhauled, you tend to fly in a faint aroma of burnt oil.

'The aircraft bucks at every hint of turbulence. Your passenger feels trussed like a chicken in helmet, goggles and straps, and isolated in the separate cockpit.

'Even moving and refuelling the aircraft makes out-of-the-ordinary athletic demands (you lift the tailskid or elevator struts and push, like a giant wheelbarrow; to reach the tank you either climb a stepladder or the cowling – there's a footstep in the fuselage to help you up).

'Yet the Tiger Moth remains popular. More than that, quite a number of pilots who have tried a lot of different aeroplanes, people who can easily afford something more upmarket, say that it's their all-time favourite aircraft.

'What makes the Tiger Moth so desirable?

'One somewhat perverse attraction is that the aircraft is so difficult to fly at all well. If you are an average 300-hour, middle-aged pilot, expect to spend five to ten hours with an instructor before reaching even basic proficiency. For the next 30 hours at least, every landing will be an adventure, and not without risk.

'The Tiger Moth will humiliate you more often than not, but just when you are exasperated and about to fall out of love, you will pull off a greaser and experience the magic sensation of touching the main-wheels and the tailskid simultaneously, so gently that the transition from air to ground passes unnoticed and you think you are still flying.

'Even the most experienced Tiger Moth pilot cannot guarantee to land like this every time. The challenge of making a perfect landing stays

ABOVE: 'Even moving and refuelling the aircraft...' *(Maxi Gainza via deHMC)*

RIGHT: ...makes out-of-the-ordinary athletic demands.' *(Maxi Gainza via deHMC)*

OPPOSITE TOP: 'An average pilot will expect to spend five to ten hours with an instructor before reaching basic proficiency. For the next 30 hours, every landing will be an adventure...' *(Brian A. Marshall)*

OPPOSITE BOTTOM: '...Then you experience the magic sensation of touching the main-wheels and tailskid simultaneously.' *(Brian A. Marshall)*

of ailerons when taxiing downwind…the best way to win at flour-bombing and spot-landing contests…how to make people laugh at air shows with crazy flying acts…the best way to tow gliders…to fly with a wingwalker…to fly a Tiger Moth with floats…there's more.

'This means you can go on learning in a Tiger Moth for years and years after you acquire one. Boredom isn't an option as long as you keep expanding your personal envelope.

'Tiger Moths get noticed, and continue to hold a place in the hearts of the British public. A Tiger Moth trundling overhead, or alighting gently on a peaceful summer's day is one of aviation's rewarding sights and, of course, a sense of history comes with the aeroplane.

'Then, as now, the Tiger Moth teaches hand, eye and feet co-ordination, and an understanding of how an aeroplane works. Furthermore, it tolerates bad techniques that would demolish many other vintage types.

'Flying in an open cockpit, and the Tiger Moth's is very open, is a big thrill, rather like the difference between riding on a motorbike and sitting inside a car.

'Most people don't realise how much they enjoyed their first Tiger Moth flight for an hour or two…and when they do, they want another.'

ABOVE: 'Tiger Moth aerobatics are…well, they're something else.' *(deHMC archive)*

BELOW: 'A sense of history comes with the aeroplane.' *(deHMC)*

with you as long as you fly Tiger Moths, adding spice to every flight.

'The same principle applies to Tiger Moth aerobatics. Loops, barrel rolls and spins are relatively easy, but a fully-axial slow roll, Immelman turn, or fully-vertical stall turn without stopping the engine…well, they are something else.

'Then there's arcane knowledge that the oldsters will pass on, like the steering effect

(Stephen Slater)

Cockpit check

1 Crash pad (leather filled with horsehair)

2 Magneto switches (on outside of cockpit)

3 Airspeed indicator

4 Altimeter

5 Fuel cut-off tap

6 Throttle and mixture controls

7 Control column

8 Turn and slip indicator

9 Rev counter

10 Oil pressure gauge

11 Rate of climb and descent indicator

12 Magnetic compass

13 Wing slot locking lever

14 Back of front seat

Note: G-ACDA is the first pre-war 1933 de Havilland School of Flying machine. It therefore features slightly different instruments to wartime Tiger Moths. They would have, for example, a 'twin needle' altimeter, a simpler airspeed indicator, a vertical oil pressure gauge and probably no rate of climb indicator.

ABOVE: The throttle lever on the left side of the cockpit is alongside an 'altitude control' lever, which controls engine mixture. Few Tiger Moths today fly high enough to warrant its use. *(Geoff Collins)*

Climb aboard

In order to fly a Tiger Moth, first you have to negotiate your way into the cockpit. At first it seems awkward, but with practice it becomes much easier. At least today's civilian pilots don't have to clamber in with those ungainly RAF parachutes attached to their bottoms. The aluminium bucket seats now have cushions where once you sat on a hard parachute pack.

The inside of each lower wing features a plywood walkway, but you avoid putting your foot close to the trailing edge of the wing, as the wood is relatively unsupported in the thin section here. Likewise, if your foot strays off the walkway there's a strong likelihood it will go straight through the fabric surface of the wing.

Squeeze two levers together and the cockpit door hinges down. There's a handhold on the back of the front cockpit to help you up. You need to treat it like mounting a horse – swing one foot into the cockpit, stand on the seat cushion and then lower yourself in.

With luck, you will now have one foot each side of the control column and resting lightly on the rudder bars. Your right hand will fall naturally on the control column, while your left hand drops equally comfortably onto the throttle lever on the left side of the cockpit. There is a mixture lever – quaintly called by de Havilland the 'altitude control' – to the right of that, but most likely it will have been disconnected. The lever itself may even have been removed, as few Tiger Moths fly high enough today to require it.

A friction nut secures the throttle in the desired position when required and ahead of that control is the fuel on/off tap, which has a spring-loaded catch to ensure the tap stays open as long as you need it to.

RIGHT: The fuel cut-off lever is connected by rods to a tap on the upper wing-mounted fuel tank. A spring-loaded catch prevents it being accidentally turned off. *(Geoff Collins)*

FAR RIGHT: The 'cheese-cutter' trim lever on the left cockpit wall controls stick loads in flight by the use of springs attached to the base of the control column. *(Geoff Collins)*

A 'cheese-cutter' trim lever is located on the left side of the cockpit. This reduces the stick loads in flight by applying a spring load to the base of the control column. It gets its nickname from its distinctive ratcheted gate.

The main instrument panel is simple, yet provides all the instruments you need. Height and airspeed are given by the two primary instruments on the left side of the panel, while the centre is dominated by a vacuum gyro-driven Reid and Sigrist Turn and Slip indicator. Its lower needle indicates the level of bank the aeroplane is maintaining – keep it in the middle and the wings are level. The upper needle indicates the balance of the aeroplane. The growl of 'stand on the needle' was a common refrain from instructors, reminding students that if the needle swung left, some more left rudder would keep the aeroplane in balance and return the needle to the centre.

The right side of the instrument panel contains the engine rev counter and oil pressure gauge. On some earlier Tiger Moths a vertical rate of climb and descent indicator was fitted, although this was deleted on many British-built wartime Tiger Moths.

A lever on the right side of the cockpit locks and unlocks the spring-loaded leading edge slots which extend from the upper wings at low

ABOVE: The instrument panel has altitude and airspeed information on the left, 'blind flying' instruments in the centre and engine instruments on the right. *(Geoff Collins)*

LEFT: A venturi on the outside of the fuselage generates a vacuum… *(Geoff Collins)*

FAR LEFT: …which in turn spins a gyroscope in the Reid and Sigrist turn indicator. Its lower needle indicates level of bank and the upper needle indicates whether the aeroplane is flying in balance. *(Geoff Collins)*

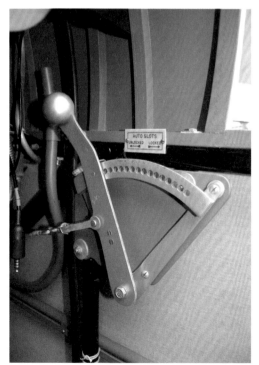

LEFT: A lever on the right side of the cockpit locks and unlocks the leading edge slots. *(Geoff Collins)*

RIGHT: The traditional P-type compass is perhaps the single most confusing item in the cockpit for pilots trained to fly modern aircraft. *(Geoff Collins)*

FAR RIGHT: The 'windy' spring-loaded airspeed indicator on the port wing strut allows the pilot to monitor airspeed while maintaining a good lookout in crowded airfield circuits.
(Geoff Collins)

airspeeds. To minimise undue wear the slots should be locked when on the ground and also during aerobatics. They are unlocked before take-off and locked after landing.

The lower centre of the panel is dominated by the P-Type compass. This is effectively a magnetic iron bar floating in a liquid-filled bowl, and therefore will always point north. A grid ring around the outside of the bowl is marked in degrees and can be turned to allow a course to be set. One then 'flies' the aeroplane onto a 'T' marked in the glass. It is possible for a confused student to fly in the exact opposite direction to that intended – some did, and some still do today!

With the exception of a modern VHF radio and intercom the remaining switches and instruments are outside the cockpit, which is actually rather sensible as that is where a Tiger Moth pilot's eyes should be. Keeping a good lookout is far more important to flight safety in a light aircraft than 'clock-watching'.

The magneto switches are in pairs on the outside of each cockpit, just ahead of the chromed brass windscreen frame. Down is off, up is on. They are positioned there so that any

member of the ground crew can see whether they are on or off before handling the propeller.

The foremost of each pair of switches controls the starboard magneto, which contains an impulse device to boost the spark to the plugs for starting. Although many pilots today simply start the aeroplane on both magnetos, it was RAF practice to start on just the starboard magneto, then flick up the port switch when the engine was running to minimise the risk of an early spark from the port magneto causing the propeller to 'kick back'.

Above the rear-seat pilot and only visible from the back cockpit is a float and sight-glass fuel gauge, while the final instrument, on the forward port interplane strut, is known as a 'Windy' airspeed indicator. It is simply a vane on a spring-loaded wire which reads against an airspeed scale on an aluminium quadrant, and is located on the wing strut to allow a student to monitor their airspeed while flying circuits around the airfield. Consequently since most circuits are flown in a left-handed pattern the indicator is positioned on the left side of the aeroplane, in the pilot's line of sight as they turn on to final approach where airspeed control is most critical.

One final challenge for a new initiate to Tiger Moth flying comes if the aircraft is fitted with a Sutton Harness. These were the standard form of seat belt from the 1930, and unlike a modern seat belt they have no buckle but instead use a locking-pin. Made of heavy canvas webbing tipped with leather, they look like something from a medieval torture chamber.

Each leather tip has a number embossed on

RIGHT: The Sutton Harness, uses a locking pin rather than a modern buckle.
(Geoff Collins)

its end. First take number 1, which has the steel locking-pin attached. Next take number 2 and lay it so that one of the reinforced eyeholes slips over the pin. Repeat the exercise with numbers 3 and 4, before inserting a spring clip in the hole at the end of the pin to secure the harness.

A single hefty pull on the pin will release the harness in an emergency. As with much else in a Tiger Moth, it looks basic but is surprisingly functional.

Walk-around check

Simply preparing, starting and taxiing the Tiger Moth takes a pilot back to a former era of flying. While it can be done safely by an individual, it is better and safer to have at least one assistant, to help with swinging the propeller and handling the wheel chocks.

A pre-flight walk-round inspection is obligatory before each flight. From a distance one can quickly appraise the obvious: are the wheel chocks in place, are the tyres properly inflated, has the cover been removed from the pitot tube on the starboard strut, have any control locking plates been removed?

From a distance, check the top surface of the upper wing. Just as importantly, is the aeroplane sitting level? If it isn't, has the previous pilot slunk away and failed to report a heavy landing?

While this section isn't intended as a detailed walk-round checklist, let's look at some of the key elements.

Ensure that the oil tank is sufficiently replenished. The dipstick is integral with the large brass filler cap. Under the engine cowling, check for any serious oil leaks, that all the throttle linkages are secure, that there is no sign of fuel leakage around the carburettor and that there aren't any stains around the cylinder heads that might indicate a leaking exhaust gasket. At the same time check that there's no damage to the propeller and that there isn't any play which would indicate loose mounting bolts.

Next, placing your left foot on the starboard

ABOVE: An integral dipstick built into the filler cap... (Geoff Collins)

LEFT: ...allows easy checking of the contents of the 2.1-gallon (9.5-litre) oil tank. (Andy Smith)

RIGHT: A step on the forward fuselage aids access... *(Geoff Collins)*

RIGHT: ...to check the contents and security of the filler cap on the upper wing-mounted fuel tank. *(Geoff Collins)*

BELOW: All flying and control surfaces, the condition of struts, control cables and bracing wires are checked. *(Geoff Collins)*

main-wheel and your right foot in the step on the fuselage, swing yourself on to the small reinforced platform on the top of the engine cowling. This allows you access to the fuel tank, which you need to 'dip' to confirm its level. Check that the filler cap is secure, and on the first flight of the day take a small sample of fuel from the drain tap at the base of the tank to check for any water contamination.

The rest of the walk-round should be used to check the airframe. You need to check its general condition, looking for damage, any split pins, or nuts which may have vibrated loose on the previous flight. The rigging wires shouldn't be bowed or slack. Cowlings and hatches should be secure. If the aeroplane is being flown solo, check that the front seat harness is secured to avoid any risk of it fouling the controls.

Clearly there will be some tension in the landing wires from the centre section to the lower wings, since they're supporting some of the weight of the wings while they're on the ground. The flying wires from the upper wing struts to the low fuselage mountings will be less rigid, since they only take up load as the aeroplane gets the air under its wings.

The wingtips, ailerons and elevators are the most prone to accidental damage, being closest to the ground. Check particularly their undersurfaces for any sign of damage or scuff marks. Finally, double-check that there isn't anything behind the aeroplane which will be damaged by propwash when the engine starts, and that there's nothing so close in front that you can't taxi safely away.

Chocks away

Checks completed, you climb aboard the aeroplane and make yourself comfortable with your harness secured. Now the ritual of starting, as old as flight itself, can begin.

There are two people involved: the pilot and the starter.

In the cockpit, the pilot selects fuel on, throttle fully closed, and moves the trim lever on the left side fully back to ease the load on the control column, which he holds back to ensure the tail doesn't rise if the engine starts with excessive revs. On the right side of the cockpit, the lever is pulled back to lock the slats in the closed position in order to prevent damage from unnecessary movement while taxiing.

From now until when the engine starts, the starter or propeller swinger is in charge of the aeroplane. He is the one at the dangerous end!

Having checked again that the chocks are in place – there are no brakes, remember – and that the switches are off, the starter opens the right-side cowling and presses a plunger on the carburettor to flood its float chamber until a small trickle of fuel is seen dribbling from the manifold drain.

Cowling secured, the starter calls 'Switches off, petrol on, throttle closed,' which, after checking, the pilot repeats back. The starter then pulls the propeller through several revolutions, most often 'four blades', to suck the mixture into the cylinders.

Next, the starter will switch on the switches ahead of the front cockpit, before calling 'Throttle set.' Again this is confirmed by the pilot, who has cracked the throttle just slightly open.

The starter then brings the propeller to just before maximum compression, before calling 'Contact.' The pilot then switches on the forward of his two magneto switches, activating the starboard magneto, and gives the thumbs up signal as well as repeating 'Contact' to confirm that the ignition is live.

The starter then pulls the blade over compression, at the same time stepping smartly backwards away from the aeroplane. As the engine fires, the pilot checks that oil pressure is rising, switches on the second magneto and adjusts the throttle to allow the engine to warm at 800–900rpm.

The Gipsy Major is normally a reliable starter. If it proves recalcitrant there are two areas to check.

If the distinctive *clunk* from the magneto's impulse mechanism cannot be heard, a sticking pawl can be freed by giving the alloy magneto drive casing a gentle tap.

If the engine has been flooded by too much fuel in the inlet system, it can be 'blown out' by turning off the ignition switches, setting full throttle and turning the engine backward to introduce air via the exhaust valves.

Of course, some engines are different to others and both the ground crewman and the pilot will learn the precise combination of 'sucking in' and throttle settings to gain success. Thus as well as teaching flying, the Tiger teaches teamwork too.

It takes four minutes to warm the Gipsy Major's 2.1 gallons (9.5 litres) of oil, so this is a good time to set the altimeter's barometric setting and check that the radio and intercom are working free of too much electrical interference. It is also a good time to adjust scarf, goggles, jacket and helmet to close out the draughts that have inevitably begun to be felt.

LEFT: The mixture is richened to start a cold engine by pressing a small brass button on the carburettor, which allows the inlet manifold to be 'flooded' with fuel. *(Andy Smith)*

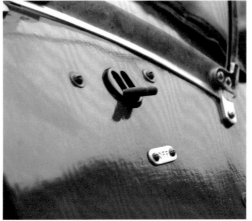

LEFT: The pilot must only switch the magnetos on once the person swinging the propeller gives the command 'Contact'. *(Geoff Collins)*

BELOW: The starboard magneto (just ahead of the fuel filter) contains the impulse device. *(Geoff Collins)*

ABOVE: As the Tiger Moth has no brakes, once the engine has warmed up it is run up to check the magnetos before taxiing. *(Andy Smith)*

BELOW: On a breezy day or in a confined space, a 'wing walker' can aid safe manoeuvring. *(Brian A. Marshall)*

Once the oil has been warmed, take a look over the shoulder to ascertain nothing is in the slipstream, check that the oil pressure is stable at 35psi and that the stick is right back and steadily advance the throttle to 1,600rpm, before switching off each magneto in turn. There should be no rough running and the drop in revs should not exceed 100rpm.

A quick burst to full throttle to check that at least 1,850rpm can be attained, then smoothly close the throttle to check that the engine will idle. A scissor-motion with both hands indicates

to the ground crewman that the chocks can be removed and the aeroplane is ready to taxi.

Time to go flying

Again, remember that the Tiger Moth has no brakes. A surprising amount of power is needed to get moving initially, then the engine is throttled back to a fast idle. The old maxim is that 'you should never taxi a Tiger Moth faster than you would walk'.

The steerable tailskid, combined with short bursts of power to blow slipstream over the rudder, makes the aeroplane surprisingly manoeuvrable on the ground. In confined spaces, a crewman exerting gentle backward pressure on a wingtip can even 'wing walk' it. This is particularly useful if you have to taxi in a crosswind, when the Tiger Moth has an embarrassing tendency to act like a weathervane and point itself into wind at every opportunity.

Above all, you must continually weave a Tiger Moth while on the ground, otherwise you *will* run into something. The aeroplane's long nose and the passenger's head blank out all of the view ahead. This taught young wartime pilots good habits from the start,

before they moved on to aeroplanes such as the Spitfire.

If space permits on the way to the end of the runway, advancing the throttle will allow a last check of the magnetos before the final pre-take-off checks. The mnemonic TTMPFFHH has been drummed into generations of pilots:

T Trim: set for take-off, by moving the 'cheese-cutter' to about two-thirds forward on its quadrant.

T Throttle: friction-nut tightened to prevent it vibrating closed if your hand is removed.

M Mixture: today normally locked fully rich.

P Propeller pitch: not applicable on a Tiger, but useful in future training.

F Fuel: confirm tap is on and that there is sufficient for the flight.

F Free slats: move the lever on the right to unlock the leading-edge slats for take-off.

H Harnesses secure.

H Hatches secure, although many larger pilots prefer to fly with the rear doors open, to give them extra shoulder room and visibility.

RIGHT: Perfect flying conditions: the wind is straight down the runway as the tail is lifted and the aeroplane accelerates. *(Geoff Collins)*

A final check that the approach and take-off paths are clear, and you line up ready for departure. A quick check with stick and rudder to ensure that you have full and free movement of the controls, a quick check of the windsock to confirm that you are into wind, and away you go.

Ease open the throttle on a count of three from idle to full power – snatching it open can result in a polite cough and a sulky silence from the old girl. Check that good engine revs and oil pressure are being attained, and at the same time push the stick gently forwards to

ABOVE LEFT: What can you see? This shot reveals the limitations of the Tiger Moth's forward visibility. *(Geoff Collins)*

BELOW: Weaving and 'putting one's head over the side' to increase visibility is a must. *(Geoff Collins)*

raise the tail. Your forward view improves, but still isn't good, so you 'sight' the aeroplane by looking down the line of the cowling to keep it straight.

A dab of rudder keeps you straight as the tail comes up, but acceleration is brisk and within no time the aeroplane feels ready to fly. Unlike some, there is no real sense of lifting the aeroplane off the ground; the Tiger simply seems to levitate, still maintaining its take-off attitude at around 70mph (120kph). After a few moments you throttle back a little to take the strain off the engine and your left foot, which has been holding left rudder to balance the aircraft against the propeller's torque and slipstream effects.

Much of the Tiger Moth's working life was spent in the circuit, so round you go, climbing through the crosswind leg and levelling out for the downwind. Once again, a mnemonic was drummed into thousands of Tiger Moth pilots' heads, pre-landing checks not always appropriate to this simple old bird but good habits for the future – BUMPFF:

B Brakes: off (there aren't any).

U Undercarriage: down (and welded there).

M Mixture: rich (still locked in place).

P Propeller pitch: fine (just as de Havilland made it).

F Fuel: on (has been all flight).

F Flaps: not fitted, of course, but check for free slats just in case they were locked closed for any aerobatics.

Wait till the end of the runway is just behind the trailing edge of the wing and turn on to base leg, then on to final approach. Close the throttle and move the trimmer almost all the way back and the speed will settle at about 65mph (105kph), with your aiming point at the end of the runway framed in the centre-section struts.

Now the aiming point is moving upwards. You're getting too low, and need a small burst of throttle. It will be considered bad form on

the ground – glide approaches make sense with a vintage aircraft, in case the engine stops on approach. Still, you can tell them you were warming the engine in case of a go-around.

If you overdo it and the aiming point disappears toward the cowling that is no problem, since the Tiger Moth side-slips beautifully. Throttle closed, left aileron, right rudder, and the airflow on the side of the aeroplane acts as a brake and she comes down like a lift.

Smooth it out now. They say that a good Tiger Moth landing starts with a good approach. You maintain a steady descent to bring you over the hedge at 50ft (15m). Keep the wings level and close the throttle. Don't think about landing, instead aim to skim along just above the runway.

Without power, the aeroplane slows…and slows. You have to pull the stick further and further back to stay in the air. You're relying on peripheral vision to keep straight and you are 'stirring the pot' with the control column as the controls get sloppier.

The aeroplane now seems ludicrously nose-high, but if you release back pressure on the stick the main-wheels will touch early and trigger a series of bounces. If that happens, open the throttle and go around again before you break something.

If you're lucky the last backward movement of the stick will coincide with the wheels and tailskid touching the ground simultaneously, a classic three-pointer. More probably the wheels will still touch early and the Tiger Moth will settle after a series of gentle hops. The landing isn't over yet, though. You need to keep the aeroplane straight with coarse rudder movements, and if there's even a hint of crosswind keep the stick into wind, deploying full aileron to prevent a gust from lifting a wing.

Clear of the runway now its 'slats locked', and trim fully back for taxiing. Don't forget to weave to see around the nose. Back at the parking area, let the engine run at a fast idle for a minute or so to allow the hot engine oil to be circulated around it.

After a final check of the magnetos at low revs you switch off, and as the engine runs down you open the throttle to prevent any risk of 'running on'. Then you close the throttle, and it's time to climb out and head for a cup of tea. But don't forget to turn off the front switches and chock the wheels first!

Tricks of the trade

The flight described above is fictional (particularly the dream three-pointer) but is typical of many Tiger Moth flights in perfect conditions. However, when the weather is fickle or the location is more challenging, the best Tiger Moth pilots will rise safely to the occasion.

Here, distilled from the experiences of many members of the de Havilland Moth Club, are a few helpful tricks of the trade.

Cockpit management

The Tiger Moth's open cockpit is possibly one of the windiest places on the planet. It is certainly not the place to try to unfold a map or plot a route.

Flying and simultaneously navigating a Tiger Moth is a far greater challenge than in an enclosed cockpit. Careful pre-flight planning can simplify much of the workload, starting with something as simple as the correct way to fold a map so that it can be read in an open cockpit.

Aviation charts are sold as plastic-coated, unfolded sheets with large white borders containing key information such as radio frequencies. Some Moth pilots cut off these borders and keep the areas containing the references separately, for easier access. It makes the folded map smaller and more manageable too.

The target in folding the map is to create three horizontal and seven vertical concertina folds, which allow sections of the map to be unfolded in flight. Each fold should be made on a flat surface and a plastic ruler should be used to create a sharp crease. The folds should be reversible, meaning they should fold either way.

The first fold is made with the chart's printed side facing down. Fold the two longest edges together to get a fold running east–west along the centre. Next open the chart and fold the lower edge up to the centre fold. Do the same

from the top edge to the centre to create the three horizontal folds running east–west across the chart.

Next reopen the chart and repeat the process making the folds north–south. This will create three horizontal and three vertical folds dividing the chart. All of the remaining folds are now north–south, further halving the three vertically folded areas and creating a concertina effect. With a 500,000:1 map folded in this way, 30 miles (50km) east–west and 50 miles (80km) north-south can be flown between each fold, and the map can be pre-folded to necessitate a minimum of manipulation in the cockpit.

Crosswinds, ground-loops and wheelers

When the Tiger Moth was first devised, airfields did not have marked runways and certainly not hard, tarmac surfaces. Therefore crosswind landings were rarely even considered. All take-offs and landings were made with reference to windsocks and simply made into wind.

The coming of marked runways for heavier aircraft with longer take-off distances made this less practicable, and pilots had to master new techniques to control tail-wheel aircraft in crosswind conditions. Put simply, the Tiger Moth doesn't like crosswinds. This results from a combination of its low landing speed, relatively narrow undercarriage, high centre of gravity (due to the top wing-mounted fuel tank), and handling traits that come from having the main-wheels ahead of that centre of gravity.

This tends to accentuate any swinging motion, meaning that the pilot has to steer continuously with rudder to keep straight during the landing run. If a swing gets out of control the inertia of the weight behind the wheels will take over, swinging the tail all the way round in a ground-loop. If that happens, there is a strong chance of overstressing the landing gear, or even of a wingtip striking the ground.

The first rule of crosswind flying in a Tiger Moth is to avoid them if at all possible. Most amateur pilots set themselves a relatively low crosswind limit. If it is above that, they do not fly. As they become more experienced they will maybe raise the limit, but only with caution.

One can often mitigate the crosswind element on a wider runway by taking off or

This sequence of shots taken was taken on a breezy day at East Kirkby in Lincolnshire. The wind was blowing from left to right across the available landing direction, and this Tiger Moth pulled off a copybook crosswind landing. The aircraft is flown as much to the downwind side of the landing area as possible and turned to 'quarter into wind' as much as possible…

As the descent is checked, the into-wind wing is kept as low as possible, to prevent it being lifted by a gust.

As the tail is lowered, full right aileron is still applied to hold down the into-wind wing. Note too that the aeroplane is needing full left rudder, to prevent it from weathercocking into the wind.
(All Brian A. Marshall)

landing at a slight diagonal from one side of the runway to the other. This also increases the into-wind component, aiding controllability.

If a strong wind is blowing directly across a take-off run, experienced Tiger Moth pilots will try to choose a take-off direction so that the wind is blowing from the left side of the aeroplane.

On full power the tendency of a Tiger Moth in calm conditions is to swing to the right due to the torque of the engine and slipstream of the propeller hitting the rudder. It therefore requires left rudder to keep straight.

With a crosswind from the left, the aeroplane has a weathercock tendency to turn into wind, which works with rather than against the available rudder control.

In any crosswind, full into-wind aileron control is needed to keep a gust from lifting the wing and putting the aeroplane into an unstable, potentially hazardous situation. In an emergency a few very experienced Tiger Moth pilots have even advocated deliberately swinging the aeroplane away from the wind, to use the weight of the fuel tank to 'pin' the wing back to the ground. Some call it clever, others folly. A far preferable solution is to avoid the situation completely.

The risk of a gust lifting a Tiger Moth wing on landing is far greater when the wings are at their highest angle of attack in the three-point attitude. The preferred attitude for a crosswind landing is therefore a 'wheeler', touching down on the main-wheels with the tail held high until the last possible moment. It has the added benefit of keeping the rudder in the airflow for longer too, increasing directional control.

The approach is made slightly faster, with some power still applied and the into-wind wing kept low to effectively side-slip the aircraft into the wind until the moment of touchdown. The theory is to level off at an altitude of a few inches while still at flying speed. A slight forward movement of the stick will then touch the main-wheels at the same time as the throttle is closed and an additional slight forward deflection of the stick will hold them on the ground.

As the aeroplane slows down the pilot continues to advance the stick in order to keep the tail up in a level-flying attitude, while at the same time working hard with the rudder to keep the aeroplane straight. Eventually, as the aircraft slows, the tail begins to sink.

By the time the tail drops to the ground the aeroplane may be at no more than a fast walking speed, but the pilot will still have to stay alert. Once again the Tiger Moth will want to behave like a weathervane and swing into the wind. A burst of power over the rudder might be required to pull it straight. There is certainly truth in the old saying that the pilot can only relax from a Tiger Moth landing once the aeroplane is back in the hangar.

Awkward starters

Swinging the propeller on the Tiger Moth is (rightly) daunting at the best of times. Some Tiger Moth pilots describe it as perhaps the highest-risk moment of any flight. It certainly requires the fullest attention of the propeller swinger and the right handling techniques. No one should attempt to swing any aircraft propeller unless they are properly trained.

The pressures on the propeller swinger increase when an engine proves reluctant to start. From cold, the Gipsy Major is normally co-operative, assuming that the *clunk* from a functioning impulse magneto can be heard as the propeller is swung, and that the correct regime of flooding the carburettor, followed by 'sucking in' for four blades, is carried out prior to turning on the switches for the start.

If the sound of the impulse mechanism is absent, it means that the drive pawl has stuck. Opening the starboard cowling and giving the alloy magneto drive casing (not the fragile Bakelite cover!) a light tap with a suitable implement usually does the trick.

If the engine has recently been run, a Gipsy Major will normal burst into life on the first or second swing, with the throttle just cracked open a fraction of an inch from the fully closed position.

The biggest challenge comes when the engine is in that grey area of being not quite cold and not quite hot. Every Tiger Moth pilot

19. Starting Procedure

The airman swinging the airscrew is always responsible for the front set of switches whether front seat is occupied or not.

Action by Occupant of Pilot's Seat	Action by Fitter
	Checks to see chocks are in place in front of wheels
	Calls "switches off, petrol on, throttle closed."
Checks switches off, turns petrol on, closes throttle, calls "Switches off, petrol on, throttle closed."	
	Floods carburettor, if engine is cold (and sucks in if necessary), calls "Throttle set."
Checks throttle lever in nearly closed position and calls "Throttle set".	
	Calls "Contact", puts impulse magneto switch (front knob of front switches) on contact (up).

Action by Occupant of Pilot's Seat	Action by Fitter
Holding stick fully back with right hand, puts impulse magneto switch (front knob of rear switches) on contact (up), calls "Contact" and keeps left hand on throttle.	
	Standing well clear checks to see elevators in "up" position, flicks over airscrew with one hand until engine fires.
When engine fires, puts rear knob of rear switches on contact.	When engine fires, puts rear knob of front switches on contact.
	If engine fails to start due to rich mixture, switches front switches off and calls "Switches off, throttle wide open, blow out"
Switches rear switches off, opens throttle fully, calls "Switches off, throttle wide open, blow out."	
	Turns airscrew backwards until cylinders are Clear of rich mixture, calls "Throttle set, contact" Puts front knob, front switch, on contact.

gets to know the vagaries of their individual aeroplane and has their patent method of getting it started.

Normally if the propeller has been swung more than eight to ten times without starting, the engine can be regarded as flooded, with excess mixture in the inlet system. The remedy for this is first to ensure that the front set of ignition switches is turned off, and call 'Switches off, full throttle, blowing out.' The pilot then ensures his switches are off too and advances the throttle to wide open before the swinger pulls the propeller backwards – in the opposite direction to normal running – for 12 blades. This allows air to be sucked in via the exhaust to clear the excess mixture.

The swinger will now call 'Throttle set,' reminding the pilot to close the throttle before, having switched on the front magneto switches, reverting to normal starting.

If that does not work, one further trick of the trade is to flood and 'suck in' the engine for four blades as if for a cold start, followed immediately by opening the throttle and 'blowing out', then starting the engine. No one seems to be able to explain why this procedure works, but it frequently does.

The right stuff

Before climbing aboard a Tiger Moth, it is important to ensure that you are suitably attired, both for comfort and safety. While many people in places such as Australia and the USA fly their Tiger Moths in summer months in T-shirts and shorts, in more temperate climes it is usual to dress more appropriately.

Modern insulated and even electrically-heated suits originally developed for microlight pilots are used by some Tiger Moth owners, but most prefer to wear more traditional flying outfits. Perhaps surprisingly, the classic 'Biggles' outfit – a good, well-fitting leather or fabric flying helmet and goggles, well-insulated but thin gloves, a warm flying jacket and a soft scarf to keep out the draught – remains just as effective as some more modern attire.

The Irvine-type flying jacket, which was the standard issue to RAF aircrew in WW2, is still used by many. Its tough leather outer coating means that many wartime-issue jackets are still in use, as well as modern reproductions. Their warm fleece lining and high collar makes them ideal in colder weather, although many pilots

ABOVE: The traditional leather flying helmet, goggles and Irvine jacket are still favoured by many, and are just as effective as more modern attire. *(Geoff Collins)*

ABOVE RIGHT: In the 1930s and 1940s, the RAF-issue one-piece 'Sidcot' suit, made of cotton lined with fleece, provided insulation against the cold. *(Richard Saward via deHMC)*

RIGHT: Some pilots prefer the added protection that military-type 'bonedomes' offer in the event of an accident. *(Geoff Collins)*

BELOW: Flying 'al fresco' like this during the war years would have been strictly against King's Regulations. However as the pilot in this case was Prince Bernhart of the Netherlands, perhaps an exception was made! *(deHMC archive)*

find them too bulky and prefer a lighter jacket for shorter summer flights.

The main role of flying equipment is to eliminate the gaps which enable cold air to get in and chill either pilot or passenger. It also has an important safety role. Protection in the event of fire is vital, therefore most pilots avoid wearing man-made fibres such as nylon, which significantly increase the risk of skin burns. It is for this reason too that most wear a military-type one-piece flying suit made of treated fireproof cotton or nomex.

These one-piece flying suits are also fitted with zip-up or Velcro-topped pockets to ensure that any items placed in them are not at risk of falling out and potentially jamming a control in flight. Many also contain kneepads and pockets designed to hold folded charts, aiding navigation in the draughty confines of a Tiger Moth cockpit.

Many pilots still use the traditional leather or canvas-type cloth helmets worn by generations of Tiger Moth crews. Though today these usually have modern headsets and microphones built into them, many people still favour the old military-style facemask, as it helps reduce wind noise over the radio microphone.

There is also a substantial school of thought in favour of 'hard' helmets, which give crews better protection against head injury in the case of an accident. Many favour former military helmets, while others use lighter helmets designed for microlight pilots.

Unless these helmets come with a particularly well-designed flip-down visor, most pilots prefer to still fly with goggles. Experience tends to indicate that the airflow curls under visors and can cause quite a degree of discomfort, particularly in the more draughty rear cockpit.

Once again, every Tiger Moth pilot has their own personal preference. Some favour the traditional 'Battle of Britain' type MkVII goggles with their distinctive twin planes of glass. Others, particularly those who wear glasses, favour ski goggles, which will comfortably fit over spectacles. Yet others use ex-military goggles. As with the different liveries borne by their Tiger Moths, such variety ensures that no two occupants will ever be dressed alike!

A wartime student's-eye view

From the diary of the late Ron Gillman DFC, DFM

Tens of thousands of wartime student pilots received their initial flying instruction on the Tiger Moth, but few have ever been able to express those early impressions as well as the late Ron Gillman. Initially serialised in *Aeroplane Monthly* magazine (www.aeroplanemonthly.com) in 1980, his memories are reproduced with thanks to its ever-enthusiastic editor Michael Oakey:

'By the end of 1940 the RAF training machine was getting into top gear, as well it might, for aircrew losses were beginning to mount and the RAF was expanding at an astonishing rate.

'I don't know how many Tiger Moths they had at the Elementary Flying Training School at Perth, but on a good day there were seldom less than 20 in the circuit at the same time, forming a continuous procession on the approach. On the tarmac the scene was alive with the crackle of Gipsy engines, the keen exhaust-tanged air being fanned into flurries as aircraft returned from the field or set off on new adventures. There was a feeling of urgency and excitement.

'The DH82 was not a difficult aircraft to handle, but not that easy to fly accurately either, and the tail-down landing technique gave a great deal of trouble. This caused a lot of anxiety, for the Chief Flying Instructor at Perth, like everywhere else, was now operating on a "get on or get out" system. If after six hours dual, a pupil still had the dexterity of a cow handling a musket, the independent checks started, and if by eight hours he was not solo or didn't look like getting away on his own in the near future, then it was back to the pool to re-muster or accept a discharge. Neither option was attractive to young men dedicated to flying aeroplanes.

'I soon got the hang of the take-offs and circuit flying, but to the onlooker most of my attempts at landing must have appeared as barely controlled crashes. I gave my instructor, Sgt Ansell, a hard time, but although he never really retaliated, there were occasions when his

distant shout in the Gosport tubes of "I've got her!" had a distinct edge to it. The engine would splutter into life to prevent the aircraft striking the earth another vicious blow, and we'd be climbing back into the sky for a further attempt.

'This problem was keeping me awake at nights, so one morning, when the lectures had finished, I made my way to the field and leaned against a hangar door, watching the stream of aircraft coming in to land. I looked particularly for the good three-pointers. They demonstrated the grace of an alighting bird, the aircraft changing attitude smoothly and continuously, denying the wheels contact with the ground until the tail was down in a near-stalled attitude, and permitting the smooth touch-down of all three points together.

'The self-imposed lesson must have sunk

ABOVE: This group of 'grading' students, photographed at Cambridge in 1939, are typical of Ron Gillman and his fellows. *(Marshall Aviation via deHMC)*

LEFT: Then as now, the relationship between student and instructor demanded a balance between tuition and confidence-building. *(deHMC)*

in, for during my hour's dual instruction that afternoon, I put down two "daisy cutters" in succession and then a third. "Good man!" piped Sgt Ansell, "Now do me another one like that!"

'I didn't, I tried to counter the last-minute sink, but it was too late. The wheels hit the ground as I was pulling back the stick. The effect was spectacular. We were launched into the air in a steep nose-up attitude. The man in the front cockpit caught the bounce, hung the aircraft on the prop and then reduced power and lowered it safely to the ground.

'The next moment we were taxiing back to the tarmac. That, I decided, was that. There were 7 hours 20 minutes dual in my log book, and I still had as much idea of flying an aeroplane as a one-armed wallpaper hanger.

'When we got back to the ramp Sgt Ansell didn't switch off, but started to climb out of the cockpit, dragging his parachute behind him. It was not unusual to change over with the engine running, and the drill was for the pupil to stay aboard until the next pupil and instructor were ready.

'I felt my body contracting within my Sidcot suit in sheer misery. There was no doubt in my mind that by the morning I would be on my way to the pool, together with another group of failures.

'My instructor was fiddling with something in the front cockpit, but I was mentally switched off. Jumping down from the catwalk he pulled the earpiece of my helmet away and shouted "OK. Off you go, and make it a good one!" My mouth opened and shut but no sound emerged. He nodded, then sauntered away to the flight office, helmet pushed to the back of his head and parachute dangling behind. His fiddling in the front cockpit must have been to secure the Sutton harness so that it couldn't foul the stick.

'I felt the control column bang my knee and looked out to see the young civilian aircraft handler waggling the aileron, indicating that he was ready to wing walk me out towards the field. As I taxied towards the airfield boundary, with a graunching of the tailskid as it negotiated the labyrinth of frozen ruts, I couldn't understand why he had sent me solo after such a performance, but there was no leather-clad helmet in the front cockpit now. It was up

BELOW: First solo. The instructor has removed his control column from the front cockpit to avoid the risk of it tangling with the seat belts. *(deHMC)*

to me. The delight at finding myself free was muted a little by a feeling of apprehension.

'On take-off, the machine fairly leapt into the air at the reduced weight, and I had to push the stick forward against the pressure of the "cheese-cutter" – the crude elevator trim – to get the speed to build up to the necessary 65mph.

'As I climbed into the circuit, concentration on the task in hand gradually diffused the feeling of anxiety. I was tasting for the first time that unique sense of freedom that only those who explore the third dimension alone can ever know.

'Ahead of me there were three other aircraft, angular dots seemingly motionless against the sky. I positioned behind the last one to follow him round.

'There was little wind and I closed the throttle on base leg at the same point as on the previous circuits. The nose swung as the torque fell away and had to be held by pressure on the rudder bar. I eased the nose down to contain the speed at the inevitable 65 and trimmed out the stick load carefully with the cheese-cutter.

'The chap in front of me was already turning on to finals, so I held my heading for a bit and then turned in on his right. The approach worked out well, the aircraft crossing the hedge at about the right height and speed. Now for the tricky bit!

'As the green and white flecked surface swam up to meet me, I hung my head over the side into the whipping slipstream and levelled off. Then came the long hiatus, the lowering whistle of the flying wires telling of the falling speed, the engine ticking over unevenly. I sensed the aircraft was about to seek the ground and started moving the stick back gently, smoothly. She's settling now. Ease the stick back, back. The nose is rising and obscuring most of the field.

'The machine seems to be hanging on the control column, poised. Now back, right back, more, and the aeroplane gives a little lurch as the tailskid touches fractionally first and she pitches gently onto the wheels. Not bad. Not bad at all!

'I relaxed totally, but too soon. The Tiger began to veer sharply to the left. I was heading for the back of the previous aircraft which was now stationary. My tailskid was sliding over the open ground. There were no brakes. I slammed the throttle open and squirmed round in the cockpit to force the rudder bar over to the right. The engine coughed once, twice, then roared. We were rushing toward the unsuspecting pupil! Then the rudder began to bite and the aircraft bounced in a skidding arc, the port wingtip missing the other fellow's tail by a few feet.

'My instructor had been watching the performance of course, despite his manner of casual indifference. He was waiting on the tarmac as I taxied in.

'"OK," he said. "A nicely-judged approach and a good touchdown, but what have I told you about the landing not being over till the aircraft's stopped? You very nearly had it there, but fortunately you took the right action. You must watch that. Every time." I was too elated to be chastened. I'd made it! First solo!

'I've often wondered why Sgt Ansell sent me solo after such an outrageous attempt at a landing, and have come to a conclusion that in his judgement I had reached the psychological point. One more like that and I would have been destroyed. He must have thought that I had just enough technique to survive, and certainly the boost to my morale did the trick. I made steady improvement from then on.

'I am eternally grateful to that man and his intuition. Training Command was full of such men. They flew long hours at a repetitive task that must have seemed doubly frustrating as it seemed endless. They gave of their expertise to clumsy young men who went on to exciting things, while they were held back because of the very nature of their skills. They created the standards that made the RAF what it was.'

Ron Gillman himself went on to a distinguished flying career, earning a DFM and DFC for low-level anti-shipping missions with Bristol Blenheim light bombers. He remained in flying post-war to become one of the first Captains with British European Airways and eventually headed their flight-training operations. Keenly involved in aviation until his passing in 1988, Captain Gillman become a regular correspondent for *Flight International* magazine, was made Master of the Guild of Air Pilots and Navigators and, perhaps most fittingly, was an enthusiastic founder member of the Vintage Aircraft Club.

'Tiger Moths were designed to be workhorses and to be flown regularly. With good routine maintenance and a little mechanical sympathy from the pilot, a Tiger Moth can go on almost indefinitely. When it does need attention, it is straightforward and simple. It is as much an engineer's as a pilot's aeroplane.'

Ian Castle
Tiger Moth engineer and restorer

Chapter Five

The engineer's view

—●—

An engineer's aeroplane

The grass runways and art-deco architecture of Sywell Aerodrome near Northampton in the English East Midlands give a clue to its history being linked with the Tiger Moth. It has been associated with DH Moths since its opening in 1928 and was, in the years before World War Two, home to the Tiger Moths of Brooklands Aviation. The tradition continues today.

LEFT: A Tiger Moth used for air experience flights undergoes routine maintenance at Sywell. *(Andy Smith)*

ABOVE: Tiger Moths used for air experience flights are maintained to rigorous Civil Aviation Authority requirements, necessitating regular inspections and overhauls.
(Geoff Collins)

During the war years as many as 120 Tiger Moths at a time were based at the airfield, either being flown by No 6 Elementary Flying Training School or serviced by engineers from Brooklands Aviation, which had a major maintenance facility there. That legacy continues at Sywell today.

As well as being home to several privately-owned Tiger Moths, Sywell is also where Ian Castle has worked for more than a decade

restoring and maintaining a fleet of Tiger Moths for experience flights. All are maintained to public transport airworthiness standards.

'We work on the same principles as an airline maintenance operation,' says Ian. 'Effectively we are the maintenance hub, where the aircraft return on a routine basis for servicing and we hold all their records here. We then schedule the winter months for deep maintenance and the annual inspections. Plus we have two aircraft under full restoration to "as new" condition. When they are ready for service, we'll rotate them with others from the fleet for a full rebuild.'

Last summer, Ian controlled the maintenance for five aircraft at a time, operating from different airfields around the UK, frequently flying more hours in a week than most privately-owned Tiger Moths fly in a year. They returned to Sywell at regular intervals on rotation for routine maintenance and checks.

'Compared with the work they did at flying schools during the war, we're not pushing them hard at all,' says Ian. 'In those days each aircraft would be flying as many as eight or ten hours a day, seven days a week. Most of it was flying circuits, with a landing every ten minutes.'

So, saying each of the Tiger Moths under Ian's supervision flew up to 50 hours in a single

RIGHT: In addition to the statutory inspection schedules, based on more than a decade of experience, Ian Castle adds some additional inspections of his own.
(Andy Smith)

week and with the majority of flights being 20- or 30-minute experience flights, that often added up to 12 flights in a day. In addition to fulfilling the inspection criteria laid down by the UK Civil Aviation Authority's LAMS (Light Aircraft Maintenance Schedule), Ian adds some additional inspections of his own.

'Because of the number of take-offs and landings we have, we check the undercarriages frequently. We check and lubricate all the undercarriage pins because that's a known wear point. We wear out tailskids too, both the mechanism and of course the iron shoe which forms its tip. Sometimes we can be replacing those on a weekly basis.'

One significant difference with the Tiger Moth's operation today is that during the war years the Tigers were being flown by inexperienced student pilots, who were inevitably hard on their aeroplanes. The pilots flying passengers today are all experienced flying instructors, some ex-Service, many with airline backgrounds and all with wide experience in flying Tiger Moths.

'Good piloting and mechanical sympathy makes a big difference in maintenance and reliability for any older aeroplane,' says Ian. 'Obviously our pilots' good landing techniques help eliminate a lot of unnecessary stresses and strains. Good engine management makes a big difference too. Not thrashing the aircraft in a slow-speed climb out, or shock-cooling the engine by slamming the throttle closed for a long glide descent, can extend the engine life significantly.'

The five Tiger Moths operated last year, despite an average age of 67 years, achieved over 98 per cent operational serviceability, a figure which would be the envy of some airlines. Ian is a big believer that regular use of an aeroplane is far more beneficial to its health than standing idle.

'I'd far rather work on an aeroplane that is regularly used, flown frequently and handled sympathetically, than even the most pristine example which spends most of its time sitting in the back of a hangar. You can get internal corrosion issues in the engine, the rigging starts to sag, seals harden and start leaking. Standing still is not good for aeroplanes. The Tiger Moth's element is in the air and that's where it needs to be.'

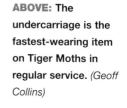

ABOVE: The undercarriage is the fastest-wearing item on Tiger Moths in regular service. *(Geoff Collins)*

LEFT: Swivel pins, even when regularly lubricated, are a known wear point. *(Geoff Collins)*

LEFT: Tailskid mechanisms are checked daily. Operation on hard tarmac or concrete surfaces causes rapid wear of the cast-iron shoes, which are often replaced weekly. *(Jonathan Elwes via deHMC)*

Routine maintenance

The Tiger Moths return to their Sywell base on average once a fortnight for a series of 50-hour and 100-hour checks. In the winter months, the extended maintenance programmes see the aircraft inspected more intensively, with bigger jobs – the overhaul of engines and replacement of 'lifed' components – being timed wherever possible to coincide. The winter maintenance also includes the annual inspections to meet CAA requirements for the Certificates of Airworthiness.

At the other end of the scale, pilots and ground crews 'in the field' carry out a series of inspections at the beginning and end of each day to ensure that the aeroplanes are in serviceable condition. These inspections are designed to highlight any potential problems and pass them on to the engineering team.

The pilot and ground crew are not authorised to carry out any maintenance work. They do, however, play an important role in ensuring that the aeroplane is serviceable and safe for the passengers. Every crewmember is encouraged to report anything with which they are unhappy.

Daily inspections

The daily inspection and routine servicing are the same as those that should be carried out by every owner. Each morning, as part of the pre-flight checks, the aircraft is given a detailed walk-round inspection, checking for any signs of wear or damage.

ABOVE: Daily inspections include checking the security of nuts, bolts and split pins that might have vibrated loose... (Andy Smith)

RIGHT: ...the security and integrity of rigging wires... (Geoff Collins)

FAR RIGHT: ...and the fabric covering for signs of splits or damage. (Geoff Collins)

Attention is given to the security of nuts, bolts or split pins that might have vibrated loose in the course of operations. Tyres are checked for wear and correct inflation. Rigging wires are checked for security and integrity, the fabric covering is checked for any splits or signs of damage.

At the rear of the aeroplane, the tail is lifted by the inner ends of the tailplane supporting struts and the steerable tailskid is checked for wear. It is also a good opportunity to check the condition of the fabric on the underside of the elevators, which, being close to the ground and in the propeller wash, can be damaged by blown debris.

The fuel tank level is checked and a small fuel sample is drained into a glass jar from the sump on the bottom to check against the presence of water. Aviation fuel contains a blue dye which contrasts with any clear water which may have contaminated it. The chances of this are increased if the aircraft has been left outside overnight, either through rain entering the tank via a leaky fuel filler seal or by condensation forming in the tank. The latter can be prevented by filling the tank at the end of each day's flying.

If water is present, being more dense than petrol it settles in the sump at the bottom of the fuel tank. Continuing to drain and sample the fuel until the water has been cleared will therefore remove the contamination.

Under the cowlings, a visual check for fuel and oil leaks is carried out and the oil level in the tank on the port side of the fuselage is checked and topped up if required. Under the starboard cowlings, the handle on the Auto-klean oil filter will be turned to operate the scraper blades which clean the elements. A check will also be made for any telltale staining on the cylinder heads, from exhaust fumes leaking from the gaskets which seal the joins to the four manifold pipes.

The propeller is checked for any chips or signs of loose sheathing and to ensure that there is no looseness of the spinner, which often warns of a slackening of the propeller retaining bolts. Next, after double-checking that the ignition switches and fuel are turned off, and that the throttle is closed and the wheel chocks are in place, the propeller is 'pulled through' several revolutions to clear any oil that

ABOVE: A fuel sample is taken from the sump at the base of the fuel tank. Any water or condensation, being heavier than petrol, will settle at the bottom of the tank, and should any be detected it can be drained off. *(Geoff Collins)*

might have drained down the cylinders and accumulated in the combustion chambers. This removes any risk of 'hydraulicing', which could wreck the engine.

Finally the cockpits and baggage areas are checked to ensure any maps or other items are securely stowed and that seats, cushions, harness and hatches are all secure.

At the end of each day's flying, the inspection process is repeated, with the addition of several large buckets of warm water and many rags, to remove mud and oil from the underside of the aeroplane and dead insects from the leading edges of the wings, rigging wires and propeller. The latter, if allowed to accumulate, can have a significant effect on aerodynamic efficiency, and their bodies contain acids which can cause corrosion.

RIGHT: The 2.1 gallons (9.5 litres) of oil in the dry-sump oil tank should be changed every three months regardless of hours flown. Even when static the oil serves an important role in absorbing acids generated by the combustion process. *(Geoff Collins)*

BELOW: A drawing showing the primary servicing points for the Gipsy Major engine. *(Maintenance and Repair Manuals, deHMC)*

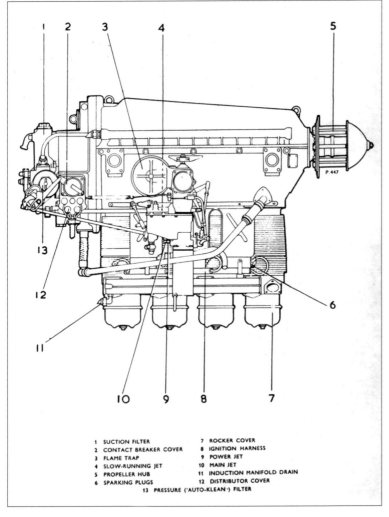

1	SUCTION FILTER	7	ROCKER COVER
2	CONTACT BREAKER COVER	8	IGNITION HARNESS
3	FLAME TRAP	9	POWER JET
4	SLOW-RUNNING JET	10	MAIN JET
5	PROPELLER HUB	11	INDUCTION MANIFOLD DRAIN
6	SPARKING PLUGS	12	DISTRIBUTOR COVER
		13	PRESSURE ('AUTO-KLEAN') FILTER

50-hour and 100-hour checks

Engine

Most privately-owned Tiger Moths fly an average of between 25 and 50 hours per year. Most engineers consequently advocate carrying out maintenance on the basis of calendar dates, rather than hours flown.

For example, it is recommended that engine oil should be changed every three months regardless of hours flown. Even when static, the oil serves an important role in absorbing acids generated by the combustion processes within the engine. While modern oils, in particular the latest semi-synthetic multigrade types, contain added corrosion inhibitors regular oil changes are the best way to minimise corrosion.

An oil change is usually the first item on the work list, ideally just after a flight. This takes advantage of the oil's lower viscosity when the engine is still warm. With a drip tray and collecting drum in place, the locking wire is removed from the drain plug at the base of the oil tank and it is unscrewed to allow the oil to drain out.

In a 100-hour inspection, the oil filter element is removed and inspected for any signs of white metal material from the engine bearings. Once this is completed it is cleaned and the element refitted in the filter.

An additional suction oil filter is fitted between the oil tank and oil inlet on the back of the engine. Its element is also removed and checked. The oil tank is then replenished with 2.1 gallons (9.5 litres) of oil and the suction oil filter primed by filling the filter casing, before checking that all the caps are secure and wire-locked in place.

Most owners use single-grade W100 oil for their engines, which contains detergent additives to dissolve carbon particles built up during combustion. Owners operating their aircraft in winter months will often use lighter-weight 80 grade oils. In the first 50 hours after an engine overhaul, non-detergent 'straight 100' oil should always be used to aid the bedding-in process.

The engine cowlings are removed, at the same time being checked for any signs of

cracking or damage. Visual checks are made of the propeller for condition and after removing the spinner, the security of the eight bolts which retain the propeller on the crankshaft.

On each side of the engine, the holding-down bolts on the engine bearers are checked for tightness and the engine mountings and bearer feet for cracks, loose nuts or other signs of damage.

The fuel tank, on/off tap and pipes are checked and the fuel filter mounted on the starboard engine bearer is dismantled and its element checked for damage or debris. A visual check is made of all the linkages between

the throttle levers in the cockpits and the carburettor, especially the ball and socket joints, for excessive wear, loose nuts or missing split pins, before all the joints, cables and bearings in the control system are lubricated.

The magneto contact breaker points are checked for the correct gaps and the impulse mechanism and cam ring are lubricated, while at the 100-hour check or winter maintenance a more thorough overhaul may be carried out. All spark plug leads are checked for condition and the plugs themselves are removed, cleaned and the electrode gaps set appropriate to the type of plug in use. Depending on condition and age, the spark plugs may be replaced at the 100-hour inspection.

With one spark plug removed from each cylinder a compression test is made on the engine to assess the condition of valves and pistons, while cylinder barrels, pushrod tubes, crankcase and cylinder heads are checked for signs of leaks or overheating. The exhaust and inlet manifolds are also checked for any signs of loose or missing retaining studs, leaking gaskets or deterioration.

With the engine cold, the rocker covers are removed from each cylinder and, after checking the cylinder holding-down nuts and rocker bracket bolts for tightness and any signs of cracking, the tappets are set.

On most Gipsy Major 1 engines both the inlet and exhaust valve clearances are set at 0.005in (0.127mm). However, on some engines which combine bronze cylinder heads with 'Mod 475' steel or duralumin pushrods to obviate the effect of carbon build-up on inlet valves, larger inlet tappet clearances are required, depending on the parts used. Engines with aluminium cylinder heads are set at 0.005in in all cases.

Once the tappet clearances have been completed the rocker covers are refilled with oil and replaced on the engine. After a final inspection of locking wires and split pins the cowlings are refitted and the inspection moves to the airframe.

Airframe

The general principles of inspection on the Tiger Moth are similar to most light aeroplanes and are enshrined in a standard inspection schedule issued by the Civil Aviation Authority, known

JACKING PADS UNDER BOTTOM LONGERONS SEE DETAIL 'A'

REAR JACKING POINT DIRECTLY UNDER TAILPLANE STAY TUBE LUGS

WOOD BLOCK TO PROTECT AXLE

JACK

METHOD OF JACKING ONE SIDE TO REMOVE WHEEL

BOTTOM LONGERON

PAD

DETAIL 'A'. LOCATION OF JACKING PADS ON BOTTOM LONGERONS

ABOVE: The correct trestling and securing of the aircraft is vital both for safety and to prevent damage to the airframe. *(Maintenance and repair handbook/deHMC)*

RIGHT: As the aircraft is close to its point of balance, a weight or a clamp should be secured to the tail to prevent it from nosing over. *(Stephen Slater)*

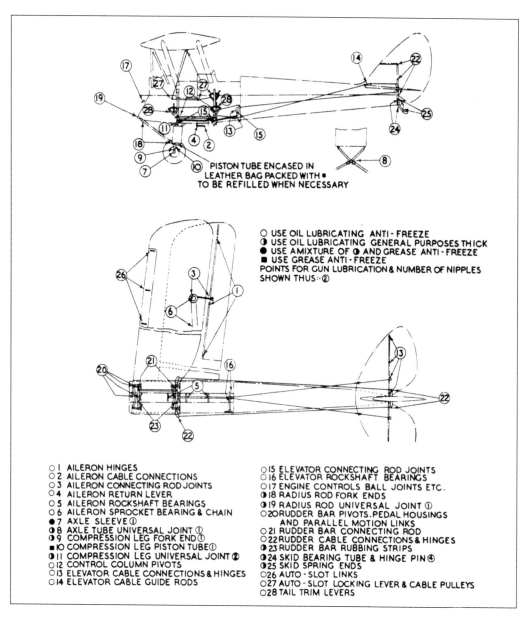

PISTON TUBE ENCASED IN
LEATHER BAG PACKED WITH ■
TO BE REFILLED WHEN NECESSARY

O USE OIL LUBRICATING ANTI-FREEZE
◑ USE OIL LUBRICATING GENERAL PURPOSES THICK
● USE A MIXTURE OF ◑ AND GREASE ANTI-FREEZE
■ USE GREASE ANTI-FREEZE
POINTS FOR GUN LUBRICATION & NUMBER OF NIPPLES
SHOWN THUS :- ②

O 1 AILERON HINGES
O 2 AILERON CABLE CONNECTIONS
O 3 AILERON CONNECTING ROD JOINTS
O 4 AILERON RETURN LEVER
O 5 AILERON ROCKSHAFT BEARINGS
O 6 AILERON SPROCKET BEARING & CHAIN
● 7 AXLE SLEEVE ①
◑ 8 AXLE TUBE UNIVERSAL JOINT ①
◑ 9 COMPRESSION LEG FORK END ①
■ 10 COMPRESSION LEG PISTON TUBE ①
◑ 11 COMPRESSION LEG UNIVERSAL JOINT ②
O 12 CONTROL COLUMN PIVOTS
O 13 ELEVATOR CABLE CONNECTIONS & HINGES
O 14 ELEVATOR CABLE GUIDE RODS
O 15 ELEVATOR CONNECTING ROD JOINTS
O 16 ELEVATOR ROCKSHAFT BEARINGS
O 17 ENGINE CONTROLS BALL JOINTS ETC.
◑ 18 RADIUS ROD FORK ENDS
◑ 19 RADIUS ROD UNIVERSAL JOINT ①
O 20 RUDDER BAR PIVOTS, PEDAL HOUSINGS
        AND PARALLEL MOTION LINKS
O 21 RUDDER BAR CONNECTING ROD
◑ 22 RUDDER CABLE CONNECTIONS & HINGES
◑ 23 RUDDER BAR RUBBING STRIPS
◑ 24 SKID BEARING TUBE & HINGE PIN ④
◑ 25 SKID SPRING ENDS
O 26 AUTO-SLOT LINKS
O 27 AUTO-SLOT LOCKING LEVER & CABLE PULLEYS
O 28 TAIL TRIM LEVERS

LEFT: This lubrication diagram shows the plethora of areas to be oiled or greased as part of the routine maintenance programme.
(Maintenance and repair handbook/deHMC)

as the LAMS or Light Aircraft Maintenance Schedule, which is applicable to all non-EASA aircraft weighing less than 2,730kg.

The basic inspection first of all ensures that the entire airframe is in a clean and undamaged condition, no bolts, locking pins or fittings are loose and that there is no excessive wear in hinges and linkages to the control surfaces.

The life of a Tiger Moth usually combines relatively short flights with grass airfields, meaning that particular emphasis should be paid to the undercarriage components. The aircraft is jacked and trestled so that it is safe and that the undercarriage is raised from the ground.

First the undercarriage structure and fittings are checked for signs of any damage or cracking. Then the top hinge bolts of the compression legs and their sockets are checked for excessive wear and the bolts replaced if necessary.

The pins which secure the divided axles and the pyramid mounting under the fuselage are likewise inspected. The wheels are removed and the hub bearings are regreased, while at the same time the wheels are checked for signs of corrosion or damage. The tailskid tube is checked for fractures and the pivot joints for wear. The cast iron tailskid shoe is checked for wear and replaced when necessary.

All inspection panels are removed from the fuselage, wing and tail surfaces, both to allow an inspection of the internal structures, lubrication of control linkages and a full inspection of all the control runs and cables. The steel tube fuselage is checked around the wing root fittings for any distortion or damage which might have been caused by a heavy landing, and the wing root fittings themselves, plus the struts and their mountings, are checked for damage or deteriorating condition.

The wooden mainplanes and tail surfaces are also checked by feeling through the fabric for signs of damaged ribs or any signs that an internal wing bracing wire may be loose or broken. The external rigging wires are closely checked for signs of corrosion or pitting and are wiped with fresh engine oil to give some added protection.

Once the checks have been completed, a ground run of the engine is carried out followed by a final check for leaks. A flight test then follows, before the aeroplane is released back to service.

Deep maintenance

In commercial operations, the more intensive maintenance activities are reserved for he winter months so as to ensure the aeroplanes' availability for revenue earning in the summer. Likewise most private owners try to schedule their maintenance for the months which offer the least clement flying weather, but the work required

varies from aeroplane to aeroplane, based on its reliability in service and the number of operating hours since the overhaul of key components such as the engine, cylinder heads or magnetos.

Experience shows that the core of a well-maintained Gipsy Major engine can comfortably attain its statutory 1,500-hour TBO (time between overhauls). Subject to inspectors' discretion and according to crankshaft modification state, they can operate 'on-condition' to 1,800 hours or more.

However, the use of leaded aviation fuels, which erode aluminium-bronze cylinder heads and their associated 'Trainer' valves, will mean that such items will normally need to be overhauled every 250 flying hours. To maintain serviceability, many aeroplanes are fitted with cylinder heads containing steel valve-seat inserts. With the older bronze-type cylinder heads owners have found that valve-seat erosion can be so severe that valves have to be 'lapped in' at intervals as short as 50 hours.

Other deep maintenance activities which are scheduled into the winter period, or even combined with a complete rebuild, sometimes include mandatory checks on components based on findings with other aircraft in service.

Only one item on a Tiger Moth is specifically 'lifed'. A mandatory requirement known as TNS29 demands the replacement of the tie rods which brace the fuselage structure at the lower wing mountings every 2,000 flying hours or 18 years, whichever is sooner. As the replacement of the components requires the removal of the aircraft wings, major work such as this is carefully co-ordinated so as to not affect the aeroplane's availability when needed.

'All aeroplanes bite fools'

Norman Jones, whose Rollason Aircraft and Engine Company probably serviced more Tiger Moths than any other organisation after World War Two, used to have that message placed on the instrument panel of every flying aeroplane that he owned. It applies equally to pilots and ground crew.

Without doubt, the most dangerous part of any aeroplane is its propeller. A cardinal rule is that regardless of the position of the ignition switches, an aircraft engine should be assumed to be 'live'. Aircraft ignition systems fail to 'safe', meaning that if a switch wire was to fall off in flight the engine would keep running. It also means, however, that if there is any problem on the ground the ignition could remain live whether the switches are on or off, and that moving the propeller could cause the engine to fire.

Equally, people can easily hurt aeroplanes. The fabric covering of a Tiger Moth can easily be torn or holed by a foot slipping off the walkway or a mishandled screwdriver slipping from one's grasp. Once it has happened, of course, all one can do is find a patch of fabric, a pot of dope and a brush and apply a patch.

Manoeuvring a Tiger Moth on the ground can also be a source of damage. The curved aluminium bows beneath the fabric on wingtips, ailerons, rudder and tail are all easily bent if inattention leads to the aircraft nudging the edge of a hangar door.

The standard method of moving a Tiger Moth if a tailskid dolly is not available is to lift the tail to shoulder height and wheel the aeroplane like a large wheelbarrow. However, if you are in the hangar how close is the top of the rudder to the roof beams or the frame of the hangar door?

If you are outside already, the aeroplane is now poised close to its centre of balance. There can be few things more embarrassing than a gust of wind catching the tail and gracefully pitching the aeroplane onto its nose!

Tiger toolkit

The history of the Tiger Moth, with an engine originally derived from a WW1 Renault design, as well as an airframe that was built all around the world, means that owners are faced with a bewildering array of nut, bolt and stud sizes during the course of even routine maintenance.

No one would consider a long journey in a 70-year-old car without carrying a toolkit – and Tiger Moth owners are no exception. Their needs can range from regular items such as a spare spark plug and the requisite spanners, to a large quantity of rags for wiping up the oil thrown out by the venerable engine. But what else do you put in the toolkit?

Leading Tiger Moth display pilot Dennis Neville, who you'll remember runs 'Captain Neville's Flying Circus', has several decades of experience of Tiger Moths and Gipsy Major engines as a pilot and engineer and was a de Havilland Engine Company apprentice. He starts with the conundrum of what spanners to use.

'What size is a spark plug spanner?' says Dennis. 'It's a good question, easiest answered by taking a sample of each type of plug used on Tiger Moths and seeing which spanners fit. I searched through my tool kit and found the following:

14mm British unscreened	$^7/_{16}$ Whit or $^{13}/_{16}$ AF or 21mm
14mm British screened	$^7/_{16}$ Whit or $^{13}/_{16}$ AF or 21mm
14mm Champion REL 37B	$^{13}/_{16}$ A/F
12mm British unscreened	$^7/_{16}$ Whit
12mm British screened	$^7/_{16}$ Whit
12mm NGK D6HA	18mm or $^3/_8$ Whit

BELOW: The tailskid dolly aids safe ground handling of the aeroplane, but a close watch has to be kept on the proximity of all four wing tips to the hangar door.
(Geoff Collins)

'As British sizes are hard to find a $^{13}/_{16}$ AF is a snug-fit alternative to a $^{7}/_{16}$ Whit and an 18mm spanner is an equally snug-fit alternative to a $^{3}/_{8}$ Whit.

'However, it's not as simple as that. All plugs require a deep socket but not all deep sockets or sockets marked 12mm or 14mm Spark Plug are deep enough to fit a screened plug. Different manufacturers machine out their plug sockets to different bores and depths.

'It follows, then, that to save a wasted journey you take a sample plug with you when you go to buy a plug spanner and try it for size. To get at the front port plug you can't afford too bulky a spanner, as the air scoop gets in the way. Consider a socket with a hexagon machined on the outside so you can get an open-ended spanner on to if necessary, or find a ring spanner with a suitable offset.

'Before you can take a screened plug out you have to disconnect the HT lead. This requires a $^{3}/_{8}$ Whit open-ended for British plugs or a $^{3}/_{4}$ AF for the American Champion spark plugs.

'Regarding other alternative spanner sizes, magneto adjustable points are listed as 4BA but 6mm is often a better fit. The contact breaker assembly is held in place by a 3BA domed bolt which will take a $^{9}/_{32}$ AF or 7mm spanner or, if the safety cut-out is fitted, a $^{1}/_{8}$ in Allen Key is required.

'Distributor covers may require 2BA, 9mm or even a $^{1}/_{8}$ Whit socket depending on whether screened and what nuts are used. For unscreened magnetos the half-knurled half-

hexagon nut requires a $^{3}/_{16}$ Whit. The thread stays the same at 2BA just to confuse!'

Spanner sizes and nut sizes can also vary depending on manufacturer. This isn't that noticeable on the larger sizes, but on the smaller sizes a few thousandths can make the difference between the spanner either fitting, or slipping and rounding off the nut. In Dennis's experience you may find you need three different spanners to adjust the points on one engine!

The cylinder heads are check-tightened with a $^{1}/_{8}$ Whit open-ended or slim combination ring. An $^{11}/_{16}$ AF may do, while you can get at some nuts with a slim-jawed crowsfoot spanner.

The oil pressure filter is released by a $1\,^{13}/_{16}$ AF single hexagon socket deep enough to clear the filter turning handle. The filter hexagon is tapered, so depending on the quality of fit several different spanner sizes will do. Originally it was a Whitworth size, probably a $1\,^{1}/_{8}$ Whit.

The suction filter is primed by removing the brass nut with a $^{5}/_{8}$ Whit open-ended or ring spanner. The exhaust and inlet manifold nuts are tightened with a $^{3}/_{16}$ Whit thin-wall socket or open-ended, while the rocker boxes are removed using a $^{3}/_{16}$ Whit open-ended and the tappets are adjusted with the same $^{3}/_{16}$ Whit open-ended or combination spanner.

While the number of tools can be daunting, so can the jargon. Dennis concludes by helping explain some of the baffling spanner and bolt sizes used:

'Whit stands for British Standard Whitworth or BSW. It has a coarser thread than British Standard Fine or BSF, but each Whit spanner will fit and probably be marked with an equivalent BSF size that will be $^{1}/_{16}$ smaller and may only be marked "BS".

'AF or A/F stands for "across flats" and is used on American threaded nuts and bolts, while BA stands for British Association and is for smaller sizes, and was used widely in electrical components – and on many Tiger Moth aircraft components.

'Whatever you do, don't think you can fit Whit or BSF nuts on the bolts on a Gipsy engine,' Dennis warns. 'De Havilland used a modified SI, metric thread form, on their piston engines, but modified the hexagonal heads of the nuts and bolts to suit British spanner sizes. It obviously seemed logical to them at the time!'

'... A flying machine deserving attention and respect, probably the most famous biplane in the world. The current generation is fortunate to have inherited so much tactile history from which to learn, before confidently passing the gauntlet on to the next.'

Stuart McKay MBE
deHMC Secretary

Epilogue

'Had there not been a world war between 1939 and 1945, what sort of light aeroplanes would enthusiastic private owners be flying now?', asks deHMC Secretary Stuart McKay. It is an impossible question to answer, of course, as the war changed almost everything, and aviation development itself was catapulted forwards at a hugely accelerated rate using the rapidly advancing technologies of the day.

LEFT: A timeless silhouette. Still charming new friends and old after more than seven decades. *(Geoff Collins)*

The de Havilland company introduced their little wooden DH60 Moth and its 60hp Cirrus engine to the world in 1925 and created a sensation and a revolution. Only two years later, as the result of suggestions from overseas agencies, they began to consider a fuselage constructed from steel tube. The greater durability of the new structure and its immediate adaptability to almost any task led directly to military interest, and the DH60M was marketed as a cheap ab initio training vehicle but with a miscellany of other functions attached: the original 'all through' trainer.

In 1938, as war clouds gathered on the European horizon and the British Government was moved to review its military resources, the Hatfield factory's Business Director took a telephone call asking if the de Havilland Company could still supply Tiger Moths. The call was from Whitehall. Another 50 aeroplanes were needed straight away and, providing engine production facilities could be reorganised quickly enough to cope, 400 more almost immediately thereafter, with the prospect for another 400 after that. The rest, as they say, is history.

If there had been no war, the Air Ministry's immediate needs for training aircraft would not have escalated into a Commonwealth requirement which totalled more than 8,000 Tiger Moths, employed for every conceivable purpose all over the world, the programme supported by a spares inventory equivalent to many times the sum total of production aircraft parts.

When the military Tiger Moth was declared obsolete in the early 1950s, the aeroplanes and enormous quantities of spares with which to support them were finally released for public consumption.

In any part of the world where Tiger Moths had been used for military training, almost every civil aviation club could offer one on the flight line with perhaps a second or more kept as a standby or source of instant replacement parts. Private ownership also blossomed as, fully overhauled and civilianised and with good engines, the aircraft were affordable to buy and to operate, with the assured back-up of spares and engineering facilities.

Hundreds of aircraft were used in the agricultural industries in Australia and New Zealand, creating a high demand for engines

and spares and pilots. But thereafter the exclusion of the Tiger Moth from such agricultural duties from the early 1960s, coupled with near saturation of the light aeroplane market by the mass export of modern production types from the USA, had a dramatic effect on the Tiger Moth population.

A generation of pilots who had known little but open-cockpit flying, no matter what the climatic conditions, were offered the prospect of enclosed cabins with heaters, shirtsleeve comfort in fast and efficient small aeroplanes with nosewheels and brakes, speed and range. Engineers learned to unscrew a damaged part and replace it with another, fresh from the factory in a box. Tiger Moths became the butt of jokes; numbers diminished as certificates were not renewed, repairs not completed; firework parties were all-consuming.

But in any interest there is a hard core of enthusiasm, which says of decline 'Enough is enough,' and the slide of the Tiger Moth towards near extinction was halted. Individuals

and small co-ownership groups took on the operation, care and maintenance of the surviving aeroplanes and recreated a demand for the regular and assured provision of consumables, restoration, overhaul and repair facilities, publications and type-specific events. A handful of organisations restarted ab initio pilot training to licence standard, with a few more providing type conversion, hire and professional joyriding.

Nobody will pretend the Tiger Moth is the easiest or the nicest aeroplane to fly, but the type has a character and needs to be told who is boss from an early stage. Very senior pilots with many command hours have been humbled by a Tiger Moth after not paying attention at every stage in flight and, just as often, before and after.

In whatever latitude, crews simply dress appropriately; sanely and sensibly in boots, suits and jackets tailored from thermally-efficient materials. Hard hats and helmets linked to modern communications equipment discretely positioned in the cockpits are necessary concessions to modern air traffic requirements; some aircraft have been fitted with brakes and tail-wheels, better to cope with hard taxiways and runways, others with self-starters and wind-driven alternators, but they are a very small minority.

People generally are curiously attracted by the aeroplane whose feel, smell, image and sound are welcoming and beckoning for new adventures. Alongside modern aircraft the Tiger Moth does not look out of place: she is not a manifestation of decrepitude, rather a flying machine deserving attention and respect; probably the most famous biplane in the world.

The current generation is fortunate to have inherited so much tactile history from which to learn, before confidently passing the gauntlet on to the next.

Stuart McKay MBE
Secretary
de Havilland Moth Club

ABOVE: Overnight stop on the deHMC Vintage Air Tour, one of the events on the Club's flying calendar.

Appendix 1

Moth ancestors and variants

Royal Aircraft Factory BE2

The prototype Royal Aircraft Factory BE2, in 1912 one of Geoffrey de Havilland's first designs, was Britain's first purpose-designed military aeroplane. Powered initially by a 70hp air-cooled Renault V-8 and later by the 90hp RAF 1a engine, the original BE2 had world-leading performance in its day, and in the hands of de Havilland in August 1912 set a new altitude record at 10,500ft (3,200m).

The BE2 was the first aircraft which could be trimmed and flown hands-off, an important asset in a reconnaissance type. In August 1914, BE2 aircraft of No 2 Squadron were deployed to St Omer in France as the 'eyes' of the British Expeditionary Force. It was the world's first overseas deployment of a military air force.

As aircraft and armament developed, the BE2's stability became a liability rather than an asset, making the type an easy target. However, it continued to be used as a rugged maid-of-all-work for the duration of the Great War. Over 4,000 examples were built between 1912 and 1917 and its layout and construction laid down the fundamentals for the Moth series of aeroplanes a decade later.

Vital statistics

Wing Span:	37ft (11.28m)
Length:	27ft 3in (8.31m)
Empty weight:	1,370lb (622kg)
Engine:	70hp Renault or 90hp RAF 1a, air-cooled V8
Cruising speed:	75mph (120kph)

Airco DH6 Trainer

While employed at Airco in 1916, de Havilland devised a strong, robust and cheap training aircraft for the Royal Flying Corps. The de Havilland DH6 was specifically designed so that it would be easy to build and repair after the mishaps common in training.

The square-cut top and bottom wings were interchangeable, while the main components of the squared-off fin and rudder were interchangeable with the tailplane and elevator. The student pilot and instructor sat in tandem in a single large open cockpit in a simple wooden box-fuselage structure.

Speed and streamlining in a basic trainer were never a priority. Despite being powered by a similar 90hp RAF 1a engine to the BE2, it was even slower! Nonetheless, over 2,200 examples

RIGHT: The BE2 was not only one of Geoffrey de Havilland's first designs, it was the first purpose-designed military aeroplane and was designed to offer 'hands-off' stability.

(Stephen Slater archive)

were built and a number survived the war to be subsequently used for joyriding, air taxis and as private aeroplanes.

The DH6 was never a glamorous type and is today almost forgotten. Yet its simple, cheap construction methods and benign handling characteristics would pave the way for the Moth a decade later.

Vital statistics

Wingspan:	35ft 11in (10.95m)
Length:	27ft 3½in (8.32m)
Empty weight:	1,460lb (663kg)
Loaded weight:	2,030lb (922kg)
Engine:	90hp (67kW) RAF 1a, air-cooled V8 engine or equivalent Curtiss OX8
Cruising speed:	70mph (113kph)

DH51

The de Havilland 51, designed in 1924, is the direct link between the military types of World War One and the smaller, lighter aircraft that created the private flying revolution of the late 1920s. Designed as an economical touring biplane, it was based on the 90hp RAF 1a engine, which was available from war-surplus stock, and used constructional methods directly evolved from types such as the BE2 and DH6.

Despite its low-cost engine, the aeroplane wasn't a commercial success. It was still too large, thirsty and cumbersome to be a good private aeroplane. Just three were sold. The sole survivor, 'Miss Kenya', returned from Africa in 1965 and is housed at the Shuttleworth Collection in Bedfordshire, where it remains the oldest flying de Havilland aeroplane in the world.

Vital statistics

Wingspan:	37ft (11.28m)
Length:	26ft 6in (8.08 m)
Empty weight:	1,342lb (609kg)
Engine:	90hp (67kW) RAF 1a, air-cooled V8 engine
Cruising speed:	90mph (145kph)

DH60 Moth

Initially powered by the ADC Cirrus – effectively one half of the ubiquitous Renault V-8 – and later by de Havilland's own Gipsy series of aero-engines, the de Havilland Moth was one of the first practical light aircraft designs to be designed for civilian training and recreational use, rather than being an adapted military design.

Smaller and lighter than the DH51, the Moth fitted the bill perfectly. By the late 1920s they were so commonplace that almost any light

biplane would be labelled a 'Moth', whether or not it was a de Havilland product.

While the wooden wing and tail structures were carried forward into the Tiger Moth, the majority of Moths utilised a wooden fuselage rather than the later steel tube structure. The most distinctive feature of earlier Moths in the air is the straight lines of the unswept wings, with none of the distinctive sweepback of the Tiger Moth.

Vital statistics (DH60G Gipsy Moth)

Wingspan:	30ft (9.15m)
Length:	23ft 11in (7.29 m)
Empty weight:	920lb (418kg)
Engine:	100hp (75kW) de Havilland Gipsy I, air-cooled 4-cylinder engine
Cruising speed:	85mph (137kph)

DH83 Fox Moth

Developed at the same time as the Tiger Moth, the DH83 Fox Moth was effectively a 'flying hansom cab', accommodating up to four passengers in a cabin ahead of the pilot's cockpit in the purpose-built plywood-skinned fuselage. A total of 154 were built in the UK, Australia and Canada and were hugely successful. The last examples remained in commercial service into the 1960s and several are still flying today.

The main components of the Fox Moth, including the wings – which were 'straightened' by changing their mountings – the engine and the undercarriage, were all similar to the Tiger Moth. The bulkier fuselage is actually more aerodynamically efficient than the Tiger's, and as a result the Fox Moth can carry a heavier load and at the same time cruise faster than its trainer equivalent.

Vital statistics

Wingspan:	30ft 10in (9.40m)
Length:	25ft 9in (7.85m)
Empty weight:	1,100lb (499kg)
Engine:	130hp (97kW) de Havilland Gipsy Major 1 or 145hp (103kW) Gipsy Major 1C, air-cooled 4-cylinder engine
Cruising speed:	100mph (160kph)

DH84 Dragon

Nicknamed by some 'the twin Fox Moth', the DH84 Dragon was designed alongside the Tiger Moth and Fox Moth as a light airliner and was introduced by Hillman's Airways on their London to Paris route in April 1933. Powered by the same Gipsy Major engines as its single-engined brethren, the design also shared similar outer-wing structures, but added a spacious wooden fuselage accommodating the pilot and up to ten passengers.

LEFT: **The DH83 Fox Moth was an 'aerial hansom cab', with a four-seat cabin ahead of the pilot. Using the same wings and engine as the Tiger Moth it could lift twice the payload and was so useful that production was restarted in Canada after WW2 to satisfy bush-flying needs.** *(Geoff Collins)*

Over 200 examples of the Dragon were built and they paved the way for other, later examples of the classic de Havilland biplane airliner, such as the later, more modern DH89 Dragon Rapide and the larger, four-engined DH86 Express.

Vital statistics

Wingspan:	47ft 4in (14.43m)
Length:	34ft 6in (10.52m)
Empty weight:	2,300lb (1,044kg)
Engine:	2 x 130hp (97kW) de Havilland Gipsy Major 1, air-cooled 4-cylinder engines
Cruising speed:	100mph (160kph)

DH82B Queen Bee

One Tiger Moth derivative with little chance of long-term survival was the DH82B Queen Bee. Based on the Tiger Moth's wings and engine, combined with the wooden fuselage from a DH60 Moth Major, it was created as a radio-controlled pilotless 'drone' for use as a gunnery target during World War Two.

Effectively one of the world's first operational unmanned aerial vehicles, the Queen Bee was guided by a radio receiver in the rear cockpit and could be flown with either conventional landing gear or fitted with floats to allow it to be retrieved from the sea at the end of a gunnery exercise. The float-equipped versions were launched by catapults using cordite charges, either from suitable cliff-top locations or from above the gun turrets of warships.

The radio control system was itself a masterpiece of ingenuity, using the best technology available at the time to pulse signals from a GPO telephone dial. Dialling '3', for example, initiated a turn to the left, '4' levelled the wings and '5' initiated a turn to the right. To land the aeroplane, the operator guided the Queen Bee into wind, and when the trailing aerial touched the surface a 'landing valve' simultaneously selected 'up' elevator to put the aeroplane into the landing attitude and earthed the ignition to stop the engine.

Of the 240 Queen Bees built, it is perhaps surprising, given their role, that more than 80 survived the war. Civilian buyers, however, believed the Queen Bee's wooden fuselage to be inferior to the metal construction of the regular Tiger Moth and were also faced with

re-equipping the rear cockpit with instruments and flying controls. By 1947 all the remaining RAF Queen Bees had been stripped for Tiger Moth spares and the wooden structures burned on bonfires.

Of the three survivors, one was shipped to the USA, where in the 1950s its spacious and largely empty rear cockpit provided the perfect camera platform for Pathé News. It is currently being restored by Bill Orbeck in Washington State. The second survivor, an example built by Scottish Aviation Limited in a converted bus garage in Glasgow, is on static display at the Mosquito Aircraft Museum at Salisbury Hall in Hertfordshire.

ABOVE: The DH84 Dragon used two Tiger Moth engines and similar wing structures mated to a spacious fuselage accommodating up to ten passengers. It was the first in a series of elegant and successful de Havilland biplane airliners. *(Geoff Collins)*

The sole flying example is now fitted with a wheel undercarriage and dual control Tiger Moth cockpits, and after restoration in the 1970s was thought to be destined for South Africa. However, the sale fell through and a syndicate known as 'The Beekeepers' was formed to share the costs of ownership and keep the aeroplane in the UK. Today, G-BLUZ is resplendent in its wartime camouflage and serial LF858, with distinctive red tips to the upper wings that once signified 'Keep Away, this aeroplane may not have a pilot!' It is truly a unique survivor.

Vital statistics

Wingspan:	29ft 4in (8.94m)
Length:	23ft 11in (7.29m)
Empty weight:	1,115lb (506kg)
Engine:	130hp (97kW) de Havilland Gipsy Major 1, air-cooled 4-cylinder engine
Cruising speed:	90mph (145kph)

Thruxton Jackaroo

Born out of necessity by an aircraft import embargo by the British government in the 1950s, and taking advantage of the plethora of war-surplus Tiger Moth airframes, the Jackaroo was developed at Thruxton aerodrome in Hampshire to create a four-seat cabin biplane. Following the flight of the first prototype in March 1957, a total of 19 aircraft were converted, three for use as crop sprayers.

The main modification involved widening the fuselage to accommodate the larger cabin, and matching the width with an extended upper wing centre section and wider-spaced undercarriage. Among the Jackaroo's quirks are that to simplify the conversion, the dual controls are not fitted to both front seats. The front and rear left-side seats are for the pilots, the right-side seats for the passengers.

Vital statistics

Wingspan:	30ft 4¼in (9.26m)
Length:	25ft (7.62m)
Empty weight:	1,360lb (617kg)
Engine:	130hp (97kW) de Havilland Gipsy Major 1, air-cooled 4-cylinder engine
Cruising speed:	90mph (145kph)

Sea Tiger

While various de Havilland Moths, Fox Moths and Tiger Moths were flown with floats in locations such as Canada and Scandinavia, and many Queen Bee derivatives were fitted with floats for their wartime role as target drones, there were few seaplanes of any type operating in post-war years in the UK. That was remedied in the 1960s when a Tiger Moth was converted for floatplane training by the Seaplane Club, an offshoot of the ubiquitous Tiger Club.

The aircraft chosen for conversion already had an auspicious history. G-AIVW had won the King's Cup Air Race in 1958. After service with the Newcastle Aero Club, it was acquired by Tiger Club 'Patron' Norman Jones and fitted with floats which had originally been installed on an Aeronca Sedan.

The 'Sea Tiger' was named 'Oswald Short' in honour of the pioneering seaplane builder and made its first flight in 1963. For almost two decades the aeroplane introduced pilots to the joys and challenges of floatplane flying, both from the sea off the South Coast of England, and later, to limit the corrosive effects of salt-water operations, from a lake near Lydd in Kent.

Sadly the Sea Tiger is no more. The aeroplane was lost in an accident in 1983, thankfully survived by its occupants. Since then no other Sea Tigers have been operated in the UK, although in Finland, the USA and Canada owners have successfully flown examples with modern lightweight GRP floats, which detract less from the aeroplane's performance and handling.

'The Sea Tiger was never the best-handling floatplane,' says Keith Sissons, who instructed pilots on the aeroplane's idiosyncrasies. 'The large floats meant that she wasn't dynamically stable and you had to work continuously to maintain balance in the turns and avoid side-slipping.

'So saying, she trained literally dozens of floatplane pilots during her time. We had great fun. Perhaps one day it might inspire another Sea Tiger to take to the water – and the air – again in the UK. There's nothing to beat messing about on floats!'

Tailpiece

While not exactly a separate variant, mention should also be made of a distinctive change to the look of Tiger Moths which for many years operated in the Netherlands.

From the 1940s, the Dutch civil aviation authorities believed that the Tiger Moth failed their requirements for stability in yaw. The result was a rather ungainly extended fin and modified rudder designed by the Fokker Company, which was required to be fitted to all Dutch civilian Tigers. Known as the *beddenplank* (bedboard), the regulations on the use of the ugly 'Fokker Tail' have only relatively recently been relaxed. It can thus be argued that European harmonisation has produced at least one favourable result.

ABOVE: A crew member acts as anchor for the original 'Sea Tiger', G-AIVW, at Lee-on-Solent in the 1970s. *(Nancy Woodall Collection via Andy Saunders)*

BELOW: What could be better than to have your own floatplane moored outside your front door? This British-registered Tiger Moth has been fitted with modern glassfibre floats by its Florida-based owner. *(Tom Beck via deHMC)*

LEFT: In 1969 Charles Boddington and his team constructed this replica of a 1914 BE2c in just 16 weeks using Tiger Moth components. *(Via Andrew King)*

MIDDLE LEFT: A few months before flying again following a five-year restoration, the 'Biggles Biplane' replica of a 1914 BE-2 shows off its uncovered Tiger Moth-based structure.. *(Tony van Geffin)*

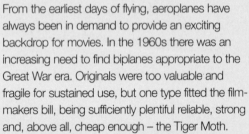

BOTTOM LEFT: Dame Judy Dench became a convert to Tiger Moths when she flew in G-ACDJ during the making of *Mrs Henderson Presents* in 2005. *(Ken Peters)*

Moths in movies

From the earliest days of flying, aeroplanes have always been in demand to provide an exciting backdrop for movies. In the 1960s there was an increasing need to find biplanes appropriate to the Great War era. Originals were too valuable and fragile for sustained use, but one type fitted the film-makers bill, being sufficiently plentiful reliable, strong and, above all, cheap enough – the Tiger Moth.

Few examples now survive of those aircraft modified to resemble Albatross, Fokker D VIIs, Curtiss Jennies and BE-2s, but one replica, nicknamed 'Biggles Biplane', is currently being restored to fly again in its movie guise. Built in 1969, it is based on a modified Tiger Moth fuselage structure, its wings re-rigged to create the authentic double-bay biplane configuration of the BE-2c.

The Biggles film which would have featured the replica was never completed. The aircraft was shipped to the USA and became part of a WW1 'Flying Circus' before being wrecked in an accident in 1977. It subsequently disappeared, but in 2005 the remains were found in New York State and it returned to the UK for restoration by Stephen Slater and Matthew Boddington. It is due to fly again in late 2009.

Tiger Moths have more recently starred in their own right, in films recreating the spirit of flying in the 1930s. Spectacular footage of a Tiger Moth flying over the Tunisian Desert marks the opening of the 1996 film *The English Patient*, while more recently Dame Judy Dench became an enthusiastic convert to Tiger Moth flying during the making of *Mrs Henderson Presents*.

Appendix 2

How many were built, and how many survive?

The information presented here is based on the records maintained by the de Havilland Moth Club, collated from the various factories around the world. However, as can be imagined, the pressures of wartime production meant that accurate records can be elusive or were destroyed. Memories too have faded over the past seven decades, and as individual Tiger Moths have circulated the globe, so yet more confusion has set in.

As a typical example, in late 1938 as many as 200 Canadian-built Tiger Moth fuselages are thought to have been shipped to the UK, where they were used to bolster the production of British-built aircraft. No records remain to confirm this; however, one fuselage bearing a serial from this batch was found on an aeroplane which was recovered from India.

Adding further to the confusion, the aeroplane was at the time owned by a Dutchman, who had bought it after it had been shipped back to Canada. The discovery was only made when the fabric was stripped off the airframe following its acquisition by a new owner from England.

DH82 Tiger Moth
Built 1931 to 1933

de Havilland, Stag Lane	114
Produced under licence in Norway	17
Produced under licence in Sweden	3
	134

DH82A Tiger Moth
Built 1933 to August 1939

de Havilland, Stag Lane and Hatfield	1,066
Norway	20
Sweden	20
Portugal	91
	1,197

DH82A Tiger Moth
Built September 1939 to August 1945

de Havilland, Hatfield	795
Morris Motors Ltd, Cowley	3,508
de Havilland Aircraft of Canada, type DH82A (CAN)	27
de Havilland Aircraft of New Zealand	345
de Havilland Aircraft Pty of Australia	1,085
	5,760

DH82C Tiger Moth
Built November 1938 to September 1942

de Havilland Aircraft of Canada	1,520
	1,520

Total	*8,611*

(Plus 420 Queen Bee aircraft built at de Havilland, Hatfield and Scottish Aviation in Glasgow.)

Known Tiger Moth survivors and locations

Recording the number of survivors is just as fraught with confusion as trying to identify the exact number built. Even today, previously unrecorded Tiger Moth 'discoveries' are being made, while at the same time some aircraft continue, sadly, to be struck off charge after accidents. However, as this manual proves, there is no such thing as an unrestorable Tiger Moth!

For the first time, based on records kept by the de Havilland Moth Club, we have attempted a breakdown of known survivors by location. Perhaps surprisingly, there are more Tiger Moths in Australia than in the UK, while New Zealand also hosts a surprising proportion of survivors.

Of course, it has to be remembered that not all of these are necessarily airworthy, nor even complete aeroplanes – deHMC Secretary Stuart McKay aptly describes them as 'whole or in pieces, real or merely dreams'. However, the survival rate is amazing and Tiger Moths do turn up in some surprisingly unusual locations!

Argentina	1
Australia	264
Belgium	20
Brazil	3
Canada	83
Chile	1
Congo	2
Denmark	8
Fiji	1
Finland	2
France	15
Germany	11
Greece	1
Iceland	1
India	12
Ireland	7
Italy	11
Malaysia	1
Malta	1
Netherlands	8
New Zealand	108
Norway	5
Papua New Guinea	1
Portugal	9
Serbia	1
South Africa	54
Spain	5
Sri Lanka	1
Sweden	15
Switzerland	5
Thailand	2
United Kingdom	241
United States	105
Zambia	1
Total	*1,006*

Appendix 3

Glossary and abbreviations

ASI Air Speed Indicator.

CAA Civil Aviation Authority.

Cabane struts Struts forming an N-shape on the forward fuselage supporting the wing centre-section and fuel tank.

CATP Commonwealth Air Training Plan.

CFS RAF Central Flying School.

'Cheese-cutter' Nickname given to the distinctive trim-control quadrant.

'Contact' Vital instruction to the propeller swinger that the ignition is live.

deHMC The de Havilland Moth Club.

DHSL de Havilland Support Limited.

EASA European Aviation Safety Agency.

EFTS Elementary Flying Training School.

Flying wires Bracing wires running upwards from lower wing roots to the top of interplane struts, distributing loads when the wings are generating lift.

ICAO International Civil Aviation Organization.

Interplane struts Supporting struts between the wings, two on each side.

Gosport tube Early cockpit intercom system, relying on similar principles to a doctor's stethoscope.

Gravity feed The use of a high-mounted fuel tank to feed fuel direct to the carburettor without the need for a pump.

LAMS Light Aircraft Maintenance Schedule.

Landing wires Bracing wires running downwards from upper cabane struts to lower wing struts, supporting the weight of the wings at rest.

Mod 112 Wartime modification to Tiger Moths to improve their recovery from spins.

PPL Private Pilot Licence.

Priming Richening the mixture by adding extra fuel to the inlet manifold to facilitate cold starting.

RAFVR Royal Air Force Volunteer Reserve.

'Scarecrow' flights Coastal patrols by unarmed light aircraft during WW2 designed to discourage U-boat activity.

Sidcot suit 1930s fleece-lined flying suit, particularly sought after for winter flying.

Sutton harness Distinctive canvas webbing seat belts, original wartime equipment.

Tailskid A hard metal shoe on a sprung mechanism at the tail of aircraft. Aids stability and shortens the landing run when used on a grass airfield.

Three-pointer A landing with the aircraft at minimum airspeed, with both main-wheels and the tailskid touching the ground simultaneously.

TMOC Tiger Moth Owners' Circle.

Wheeler A landing at slightly higher speed than a three-pointer, on both main-wheels, holding the tail off the ground. Provides additional control in crosswinds and saves tailskid wear on asphalt runways.

Appendix 4

Useful contacts

This is just a small selection of the many suppliers worldwide. A fuller list can be found in the Moth Service Register on the de Havilland Moth Club website at www.dhmothclub.co.uk.

Tiger Moth flights and flying lessons

Cambridge Flying Group
The Airport
Newmarket Road
Cambridge
CB5 8RX
United Kingdom
Tel +44 1223 293 343
email info@cambridgeflyinggroup.co.uk

Classic Wings
Imperial War Museum
Duxford
Cambridgeshire CB2 4QR
United Kingdom
Tel +44 870 902 6146
email info@classic-wings.co.uk

Plane Heritage Ltd
47 School Hill
Storrington
West Sussex
RH20 4NA
England
Tel +44 5601 623143
email info@planeheritage.com

The Tiger Club
Headcorn Aerodrome
Headcorn
Ashford
Kent
TN27 9HX
United Kingdom
Tel +44 1622 891 017
email info@tigerclub.co.uk

Henlow Flying Club
Joe Wright
c/o RAF Henlow
Bedfordshire SG16 6DN
Tel +44 1462 851 936
Henlow Flying Club offers trial flights and PPL training in aircraft including the Chipmunk in which Prince Charles learned to fly and Tiger Moth G-APAP.

South Coast Flying Club
Old Noarlunga Airfield
Port Noarlunga South
Nr Adelaide
South Australia
Tel +61 8 8382 6295

New Zealand Sport and Vintage Aviation Society
PO Box 669
Hood Aerodrome
Masterton
New Zealand
Tel +64 6 377 3466
email: svas@wise.net.nz
A non-profit organisation formed in 1976 for restoring and maintaining vintage aircraft. It offers tail-wheel (or skid) conversions to PPL-qualified pilots. The fleet presently includes two Tiger Moths, a J3 Cub and a Percival Proctor 5.

Tiger Moth World Adventure Park
Torquay Airport
325 Blackgate Road, Torquay
Vic 3228
Australia
Tel +61 3 5261 5100
Website www.tigermothworld.com

Vintage Tiger Moth Flights
Martiens Steyn
13 Waterbessiesstreet
Roodepoort (Johannesburg) 1734
South Africa
Tel +27 837 766 667

Tiger Moth restoration and maintenance

Aero Antiques
Ron Souch
Durley Airstrip
Hill Farm
Netherhill Lane Durley
Nr Southampton
Hampshire SO32 4BP
United Kingdom
Tel/fax +44 1489 789 829

Matthew Boddington
Sywell Aerodrome
Northamptonshire NN6 0BN
United Kingdom
email matthew@theboddingtons.co.uk

BBAES
Ben Borsberry
24 Woodlands Road
Sonning Common
Reading
Berkshire RG4 9TE
United Kingdom
Tel +44 1189 723583

Classique Aéro Service
Patrick Siegwald
Aérodrome d'Orbigny
Les Pallis
37460 Orbigny
France
Tel +33 2 47 94 20 52
email classiqueaeroservice@free.fr

Crofton Aeroplane Services
Paul Groves
31 Russell Road
Lee-on-Solent
Hampshire PO13 9HR
United Kingdom
Tel +44 2392 551 870
email grovesmoth@ntlworld.com

Croydon Aircraft Company
Colin Smith Old Mandeville Airfield
Gore
New Zealand
email croydon.aircraft@esi.co.nz

Henry Labouchere
Bluetile Farm House
Field Dalling
Holt
Norfolk NR25 7AS
United Kingdom
Tel +44 1328 830 003

Ian Castle
Sywell Aerodrome
Northamptonshire
NN6 0BN
United Kingdom
Tel +44 1604 492 222

Mothcair Aviation Services
The Airfield
Murwillumbah
NSW 2484
Australia
Tel/fax +61 2 6672 1592

Newbury Aeroplane Company
Jan Cooper
Denford Manor
Hungerford
Berkshire
RG17 0UN
United Kingdom
email jan@newburyaeroplanecompany.co.uk

Skysport Engineering Ltd
Tim Moore
Rotary Farm
Thorncote Green
Nr Hatch, Sandy
Bedfordshire
SG19 1PU
United Kingdom
email skysporteng@aol.com

The Incredible Cloth Flying Machine Company
Arthur Mason
31 North End Road
Quainton
Buckinghamshire
HP22 4BD
United Kingdom
email arthur.mason@tiscali.net
Wood and fabric repairs.

de Havilland Support Limited
Building 213
Duxford Airfield
Cambridgeshire
CB2 4QR
United Kingdom
Tel +44 (0) 1223 830090

Engine specialists

Deltair Airmotive Ltd
17 Aston Road
Waterlooville
Hampshire
PO7 7XG
United Kingdom
Tel +44 239 225 5255
email sales@deltair-airmotive.com

Vintage Engine Technology Ltd
Little Gransden Airfield
Sandy
Bedfordshire
SG19 3BP
United Kingdom
Tel +44 1767 651 794

Aircraft-grade timber

Davidson Aeroworks
Neil Davidson
2135 St Mary Lake Road
Kimberley
British Columbia V1A 3K4
Canada
Tel +1 250 427 7178
email peggneil@xplornet.com
Supplier of Canadian Spruce wing spars and
other wooden components, internal wing
bracing wires and fittings.

Dudley Pattison
Swindon Aircraft Timber Company
Field Rise
Kite Hill
Wanborough
Wiltshire
SN4 0AW
United Kingdom
Tel +44 1793 791 517

Fabric, dope and adhesives

Aircraft Spruce & Specialty Ltd
225 Airport Circle
Corona
CA 92880
USA
Tel +1 951 372 9555

LAS Aerospace Ltd
Okehampton
Devon
EX20 1UA
United Kingdom
Tel +44 1837 658 081
Website www.lasaero.com

Skycraft Ltd
Dave Almey
Spalding
Lincolnshire
PE12 6DP
United Kingdom
Tel 01406 371779

Rigging wires

Bruntons Aero Components Ltd
Inveresk Industrial Estate
Musselburgh
East Lothian
EH1 7PA
United Kingdom
Tel 0131 665 3888
Website www.bruntons.co.uk

All things de Havilland Moth

de Havilland Moth Club
Staggers
23 Hall Park Hill
Berkhamsted
Hertfordshire
HP4 2NH
United Kingdom
Tel/fax 01442 862077
email dhmothclub@dhmothclub.co.uk

Index

A&AEE Martlesham Heath 23, 25
Aerobatics 50, 95-97, 108
Aero engines
    ADC Cirrus 18, 20, 54, 144, 147
    de Havilland
        Gipsy I 12-13, 19-21, 25, 53-54, 147
        Gipsy III 21, 25
        Gipsy Major 1 13, 25, 26, 32,
            54-56, 115, 121, 139-140, 148
        Gipsy Major 1C 33, 56, 59, 95 102
        Gipsy Major 1F 56, 59
        Gypsy Major 10 55
        Holden Motors 32
        Menasco Pirate 33
        RAF 1a V8 18, 54, 146-147
        Renault V8 54, 146-147
Ailerons 14, 23, 28, 48-50, 72, 82, 85,
    97, 108, 114, 120-121
Air Askari Corps 32
Air Battalion of the Royal Engineers 42
Airco 17, 42
    DH4 17, 42
    DH6 18, 42, 146-147
    DH9 17, 42
Airdisco 18
Air Ministry 17, 19, 23-24, 26-27, 33, 144
    Pilots Notes 122
Air racing 95
Ansell, Sgt 124, 126
Anti-spin strakes 28
Armament 29
Auster 55
Avro
    Avian 19
    Tutor 22

BAE Systems 40, 52
Baggage compartment 48, 133
Barton, Bernard 52
Bedford, Lord Tavistock, Duke of 39
Bedford, Mary, Lady Tavistock, Duchess
    of 39
Beekeepers Flying Group 150
Benjamin, Lewis 97-98
Bernhart, Prince of the Netherlands 123
Biddle, Richard 87
Bishop, C. Nepean 37, 95

Blackburn Bluebird 19
Blind flying 27, 111
Bloom, Nick 106
Boddington, Charles 152
Boddington, Matthew 66, 71, 152
Bowker, Bill 36
Brancker, Sir Sefton 19
Bristol Fighter 13
British Aerospace 40, 52
British Commonwealth Air Training
    Plan 32
Broad, Hubert 20-21, 23
Brooklands Aviation 130
Bruce, J. M. 29
Butler, Alan Samuel 43
Buying 101-103

Cambridge airfield/airport 19, 94
Cambridge Flying Group 94, 99
Captain Neville's Flying Cirrus 98, 140
Castle, Ian 128, 130
Centre of gravity 23, 28
Certificate of Airworthiness 52, 102, 132
Chocks 14, 48, 113-114, 119
Civil Aviation Authority 55, 97, 130,
    132, 136
    Display Authorisation 97
    Light Aircraft Maintenance Schedule
        (LAMS) 131, 137
Coastal Patrol Flights 27, 29
Cobham, Sir Alan 24-25
Cockpit check 109
Cockpits 47, 103, 110-111, 124
    communication (Gosport tubes) 28, 125
    enclosed 32
    floor 30, 82
    front 27, 47
    management 119
    seat harness 112-114
Collingwood Classic Aircraft
    Foundation 94
Colour schemes 12, 31, 33, 124, 150
Cooper, Jan 87
Costs of ownership 91-92
    engine rebuilds 102
    hangarage 92
    re-rigging 103

Crop dusting 35
Crosswind landings 14, 119-121
Crystal Palace Engineering School 41
Cyster, David 99

Deep maintenance 138-139
de Havilland, Charles 41
de Havilland, Geoffrey 10, 17-19, 23,
    40-42, 146
    knighthood 43
de Havilland, Geoffrey Jnr 20, 43
de Havilland, Joan 43
de Havilland, John 43
de Havilland, Ione 41
de Havilland, Ivon 41
de Havilland, Louise 42-43
de Havilland Aircraft Co. 18, 40-41, 43,
    92, 144
    DH51 18, 146
    DH53 Hummingbird 18
    DH60 Cirrus Moth 20
    DH60 Moth 10, 18, 20-21, 24, 38,
        43, 52, 67, 140, 147-148
    DH60G Gipsy Moth 20-21, 148
    DH60GIII Moth Major 21, 103, 149
    DH60M Metal Moth 21
    DH60T Moth Trainer 21, 23
    DH60X Hermes Moth 20
    DH71 Tiger Moth 20
    DH80A Puss Moth 39
    DH82 Tiger Moth 23-25
        maiden flight 23
    DH82A Tiger Moth et seq.
        ambulance conversion 33
        Biggles Biplane 152
        first production aircraft 25-26,
            87, 109
        replica WW1 aircraft 152
        Sea Tiger 150-151
        Tiger Moth Mk II 26
    DH82B Queen Bee 47, 149-150,
        153
    DH83 Fox Moth 148
    DH84 Dragon 38, 43, 148-149
    DH86 Express 43, 149
    DH87 Hornet Moth 29, 39
    DH88 Comet racer 43

DH89 Dragon Rapide 38-39, 43,
   52, 149
DH90 Dragonfly 38
DH98 Mosquito 29, 43, 67, 80
DH100 Vampire 43
DH104 Dove 52
DH106 Comet 43
DH108 Swallow 43
DH114 Heron 52
DH121 Trident 41
DH125 41
de Havilland Canada
   DHC-1 Chipmunk 14, 35, 52, 55, 98
   DH82C Tiger Moth 32-33, 153
de Havilland Engine Co. 98, 140
de Havilland Moth Club (deHMC) 38-40,
   78, 91-92, 100-101, 119
   Electric Moth e-mails 40
   Flying Duchess Trophy 39
   Little Gransden Rally 1976 39
   Moth Forum 40
   Moth Minor newsletter 40
   Technical Support Group (TSG) 40
   The Moth magazine 40, 101
   Vintage Air Tour 145
   website 40
   Woburn Abbey Moth Rally 39;
      1980 39; 2005 100
de Havilland Support Ltd (DHSL) 40, 52
Deltair Airmotive 55
Dench, Dame Judy 152
Diamond Nine formation team 100

European Aviation Safety Agency
   (EASA) 55
Elwes, Jonathan 99
Engine 22, 48, 53-62, 102, 133-136, 157
   carburettors 18, 61-62, 114-115, 121
   compression ratio 56
   cooling system 58-60
   crankcase 56, 58-59
   crankshaft 56-57, 102
   cylinder barrels 56, 58-59
   cylinder head 55, 59-61, 139
   exhaust system 60, 136
   fuel system 54, 61, 95, 110, 113,
      133, 135, 139
   lubrication system 56-58, 61
   oil system 54-55, 58, 61, 103, 113,
      115-116, 133-134
   pistons 59
   servicing points 134
Engine cowlings 48, 103, 114, 121, 134
English Patient, The film 152

Experience flights 37, 92, 129-131
Export sales 24

Fabric covering 30-31, 73-76, 85-86,
   103, 132-133, 140
Famous Grouse Rally 39
Farm Aviation 36
Farman 41
Fiennes, Roger 99
Finch-Hatton, Denys 92
Fleet Air Arm 37
Floatplanes 95, 108, 150-151
Flying characteristics 13-14, 48, 50,
   106, 145
   landing 106, 118, 124
   spinning 28
Flying controls and instruments 28, 30,
   35, 47, 103, 109-112, 138
   illumination 28
   instrument panel 35, 109
Flying outfits and equipment 23, 106,
   122-124, 145
Flying schools 155
   de Havilland School of Flying,
      Hatfield 25-26, 35, 37, 87, 109
   EFTS 26-28, 33, 130
   ERFTS 26-27, 33
   Hatfield Reserve 8
   Marshalls Flying School,
      Cambridge 35
   RAF Central Flying School 25, 100
   Service Flying Training Schools 27
   University Air Squadrons 26, 33-34
   No 3 Flying Training School,
      Grantham 24
Ford, Paul 71
Formation flying 95, 100-101
Fuel tank 14, 26, 30, 48, 61, 73, 95,
   110, 114, 119, 133, 135
Fuselage 26, 30, 46-48, 64-67, 70, 103,
   140
   accident damage 67
   tie bars 139

Gallais, Viscount Yves le 35
Gillman DFC, DFM, Ron 124-127
Ground loops 119

Hagg, Arthur 23
Halford, Major Frank 18-19
Hall, Charles 27
Hawker Siddeley Aviation 40, 52
Hawker Tomtit 23
Hearle, Frank 41-42

Hinckler, Bert 99
Hope, Wally 21
Hughes, Bryn 87
Hunter, Douglas 23

Ignition system 48, 62-64, 122, 133,
   135-136, 140
   magnetos 18, 48, 62, 112, 115-117,
      121, 135-136
Imperial War Museum, Duxford 52
Inspections 130, 132-138
   after-flight and cleaning 133
   daily 132-133
   pre-flight walk-around check
      113-114, 132
   pre-landing checks 118
   50 and 100-hour checks 132, 134,
      136
Insurance 97
International Civil Aviation Organisation
   (ICAO) 52
Ison, Bill 94

Johnson, Amy 20
Jodel 38, 101
Jones, Norman 37, 140, 150

King's Cup Air Race 1926-28 21;
   1958 150

Labouchere, Colin 95
Lecomber, Brian 91
Limbo flying 92, 98
Long-distance flights 99
Lowdell, Sq Ldr George 28-29
Lubrication diagram 137

MacRobertson air race 1934 43
Maintenance and repair
   manuals 15, 52, 55
Markham, Barry 99
Markham, Beryl 92
Marshall, Arthur 19
McKay MBE, Stuart 38, 40, 143-145,
   153
Milsom, Jeff 100
Mosquito Aircraft Museum, Salisbury
   Hall 149
Moth Club of Switzerland 103
Motor Omnibus Construction Co. 41
Mrs Henderson Presents film 152

National Aviation Days 25
Neville, Dennis 98, 140-141

Neville, Tricia 98
Newark Air Museum 49
Newcastle Aero Club 150
New Zealand Sport and Vintage Aviation
    Society 94
Night flying 28
Nuffield, Lord 30

O'Gorman, Mervyn 42
Orbeck, Bill 149
Owning groups 91, 145

Page, Sir Frederick Handley 50
Paraslasher 28-29
Parkhouse, Nick 99
Penrose, Desmond 40
Percival Prentice 35
Pitts Special 97
Poncelet, Roger 80
Private Pilot's Licence 94
Production 12, 33, 47, 89 144, 153
    Australia 32-33, 65, 72, 153
    Canada 32-33, 48, 68-69, 72
    Hatfield factory 12, 26-27, 40, 43,
        47, 144, 153
    India 32
    Morris Motors, Cowley 29-31,
        47, 153
    New Zealand 32-33, 153
    Norway 24, 153
    Portugal 153
    Stag Lane factory 24, 153
    Sweden 153
Propeller 62, 78-80, 113, 133,
    135, 140
Propeller swinger (starter) 14, 48,
    114-115, 121-122
Purchase prices 14-15, 33, 101-103

Radio equipment 28, 48
RAF Museum 29
Refuelling 106
Reid, Sq Ldr George 28
Repairs 52, 67, 84-87
Rigging 31, 50, 76-78, 102, 114, 132-
    133, 157
    flying wires 50, 71, 77, 114
    incidence wires 77
    landing wires 50, 71, 77, 114
    truing 31, 50
Rollason Aircraft and Engines 35-37,
    140
Routine maintenance 130, 135,
    137-138, 156

Royal Aero Club 17
Royal Aircraft Factory, Farnborough 17,
    41-42
    BE1 42
    BE2 18, 42, 146, 152
    FE2 42
Royal Air Force (RAF) 21, 26-27, 32, 50
    Air Training Plan 26
    Halton 39
    Henlow 87, 92, 150
    Kemble 87
    Larkhill 9
    Training Command 127
    No 81 Squadron 28
Royal Air Force Volunteer Reserve
    (RAFVR) 14-15, 26, 33-34, 94, 98
Royal Canadian Air Force 14
Royal Navy 27, 37
    Britannia Flight, Dartmouth 37
    HMS Eagle 37
    HMS Pursuer 33, 35
Royal Swedish Aero Club 24

SAAB 24
Scarecrow anti-submarine patrols – see
    Coastal Patrol Flights
Scottish Aviation Ltd 149, 153
Seaplane Club 150
Seven Barrows flying field, Newbury 42
Sharman, Paul 55
Shea-Simmons, Charles 100
Shell Aviation Department 39
Shuttleworth Vintage Aviation Society
    and Collection 94, 147
Silk, Cathy 89
Sissons, Keith 151
Slater, Stephen 152
Sopwith Camel 14
Spanner sizes and threads 140-141
Stag Lane factory and aerodrome,
    Edgware 19, 23, 43
Starting 14, 113-114, 121-122
Survivors 12, 89, 153
    locations by country 153
    oldest 24
Swedish Air Force 21, 24
Sywell Aerodrome 129, 132

Tailskid dolly 140
Tail unit 30, 47, 70, 76, 81-82, 133, 138
    elevators 14, 73, 82, 114, 133
    fin 73
    rudder 73
    tailplane 73

Taxiing and ground handling 14, 23, 50,
    108, 113, 116-118, 140
Tempest, Barry 95-98
Thomas, George Holt 42-43
Thruxton Jackeroo 39, 94, 98, 150
Tiger Club 37, 45, 95, 98, 150
    The Barnstormers 37, 96
    Super Tigers 95, 97
Tiger Moth Owner's Circle (TOMC)
    38-39
Tiger Nine formation team 9, 100-101
Toolkit 140-141
Trestling the airframe 136

Undercarriage 14, 31, 67-70, 102-103,
    131, 137
    Canadian aircraft 33
    Fokker Tail 151
    main wheel brakes 14, 33
    tailskid 14, 68, 73, 116, 131, 137
    tail wheel 14, 33, 68-69, 145
    tyres 69, 113, 133
    wheels 68

Vaisey, Mike 55
Vintage Aircraft Club 127
Vintech 55, 57, 63
Vonlathen, Bruno 103

War Office 42
Willans & Robinson 41
Williams, Neil 95
Willies, Bob 14
Wings (mainplanes) 47-50, 70-73,
    76-77, 81-84, 102, 114, 138
    bracing wires 70-72, 114
    control cables 72, 78, 114
    dihedral 23
    leading edge slats 50 72, 111
    lower wings 23, 72, 77, 110
    ribs 31, 70-71, 75, 83-85
    spars 23, 31, 70-71, 84
    stagger 10, 23, 77
    struts 30, 50, 70, 72-73
    sweepback 10, 23, 73
    upper wings 10, 23, 50, 72, 77
    wingspan 73
    wingtips 72, 85-86, 114
Wing walkers 97-98, 108
Wolseley 41
Woodwork 70-73, 80-85
    aircraft-quality timber 71, 81, 157
    quarter sawing 82-83
Wright Brothers 41, 70